Do Not Love Your Neighbour as Yourself?

Law and Religion

Volumes published in this Brill Research Perspectives title are listed at *brill.com/rplrs*

Do Not Love Your Neighbour as Yourself?

The Role of Neighbourly Love in Law, Theology of Law, and Church Polity

By

Leon van den Broeke

BRILL

LEIDEN | BOSTON

Library of Congress Control Number: 2024952732

Typeface for the Latin, Greek, and Cyrillic scripts: "Brill". See and download: brill.com/brill-typeface.

ISSN 2468-2985
ISBN 978-90-04-67996-2 (paperback)
ISBN 978-90-04-67997-9 (e-book)
DOI 10.1163/9789004679979

This book is printed on acid-free paper and produced in a sustainable manner.

Contents

Preface

'There is no part of jurisprudence that contributes more to the prosperity of State and Church, indeed to the happiness of all mankind, than precisely a well-ordered and thorough knowledge of church law', said Groningen professor in law Frederik Adolf van der Marck (1719–1800).[1] Reformed church polity scholar Frederik L. Rutgers (1836–1917) included this quote in his 1889 speech about the validity of the old church order of the Dutch Reformed Churches. He appreciated Van der Marck's efforts for church polity in a time of decline.[2] Church polity, then, is a happiness maker.

After some years of preparation, the board of the Theological University Kampen | Utrecht, the Netherlands, appointed me on 1 February 2021 as Extraordinary Professor Theology of Law and Church Polity in the Context of Religion and Society. On 10 December 2021 I gave my inaugural address on the right of the other in theology of law, law, and church polity. The ceremony was limited due to the COVID-9 context. Nevertheless, we were able to have the ceremony, and I was able to deliver this address. The extended lecture was printed in Dutch. In view of an international audience, this lecture has been translated into English. This English manuscript is an elaboration and revision from the Dutch text.

The day of my inauguration was in the time of Advent. The Christian faith community lives with an expectation of the future. This involves people, like the workers in the vineyard working the vineyard and bring in the harvest. In doing so, our task is not only to look after our own interest, but also that of our neighbour, in all reciprocity. The Church Father Augustine of Hippo (354–430) stressed the importance of good works while putting it into perspective: 'We

---

1 J. Kuyk, "Marck, Frederik Adolf, van der," in *Nieuw Nederlandsch Biografisch Woordenboek* 3, eds. P.C. Molhuysen and P.J. Blok (Leiden: A.W. Sijthoff, 1914), 816–819; 'Nulla jurisprudentiae pars salutem Reipublicae et Ecclesiae, immo totius generis humani felicitatem magis amplificat, quam quidem distinctior et pro-fundior juris Ecclesiastici scientia'; Frederik A. van der Marck. *Lectiones Academicae.* tom. II, fascic. III (Groningae: Hajo Spandaw, 1771–1776), 248ff. F.L. Rutgers noemt dit citaat van Van der Marck in zijn: *De geldigheid van de oude Kerkenordening der Nederlandsche Gereformeerde Kerken: Rede, gehouden bij de overdracht van het Rectoraat der Vrije Universiteit, den 21 October 1889.* Met aanteekeningen en aktenstukken (Amsterdam: J.A. Wormser, 1890), 6.

2 'Van de bovengenoemde "Lectiones Academicae" behandelt het eerste Deel (Ed. 1771): "Selecta philosophiae practicae jurisque naturae capita et praecipue officia erga Deum;" en het tweede Deel, in drie Stukken, alle in omvang met Deelen gelijkstaande (ed. 1772, 1775 en 1776): "Praecipua juris ecclesiastici Protestantium universalis capita"'; Rutgers, *De geldigheid van de oude Kerkenordening*, 6.

do good works not only for the benefit of others. We also benefit ourselves.'[3] So it is with charity: it is loving the other as yourself. Charity ultimately does us good. In putting it into practice, we ourselves are also in the picture. In it and with it, justice is done and something of peace is created. This corresponds with the Psalm for the third Sunday of Advent, which bears the Latin name *Gaudete* (Rejoice) two days after my inaugural lecture. Verse 11 from Psalm 85 maintains: 'Love and faithfulness meet together; righteousness and peace kiss each other.'[4]

I would like to express my gratitude to Matthew van Maastricht for his kind assistance with my grammar and to Prof. Bart van Klink (the Netherlands), who was willing to cast his positive-critical eye over the draft oration. And to Lauren Danahy and Akiko Hakuno, Brill | Nijhoff for their kind help and guiding me through the editorial process in this series. Also, I would like to thank the chief editors and my esteemed colleagues Norman Doe and John Witte Jr. for accepting this book in this Brill series.

Leon van den Broeke
Summer 2024

3 In Dutch: 'We verrichten goede werken niet alleen ten behoeve van de ander. We worden er zelf ook beter van'; *Sermo* 38, 8; Aurelius Augustinus, *Schatkamer van het geloof: Preken over teksten uit het Oude Testament* [*Sermones de scripturis 1–50*], eds. Joost van Neer, Martijn Schrama OSA and Anke Tigchelaar (Budel: Damon, 2013).

4 Bible Study Tools, "New International Version (NIV)," accessed 24 September 2024, https://www.biblestudytools.com/psalms/85.html.

Abbreviations

CCMW	Centre for Church and Mission in the West
DCL	Dutch Civil Law
GKv	*Gereformeerde Kerken vrijgemaakt* (Reformed Churches liberated)
ICCPR	International Covenant on Civil and Political Rights
UDHR	Universal Declaration of Human Rights

Do Not Love Your Neighbour as Yourself?

The Role of Neighbourly Love in Law, Theology of Law, and Church Polity

Leon van den Broeke
Theological University Utrecht, The Netherlands
leon.vandenbroeke@tuu.nl

Abstract

This book explores the notion of neighbourly law. In the twentieth century, some German church law scholars viewed neighbour law as the foundational principle of the church law system. However, this perspective has since evolved. Around the year 2000, there was a growing focus in the Anglo-Saxon world on the relationship between love and law. Although neighbour law can no longer be regarded as the sole foundation of church law, the obligation remains to reflect critically on the role of the neighbour in legal theological discourse, the development and codification of church law, and its practical application. Canon law is a diaconal ordering of God's love, or neighbour law.

Keywords

neighbourly law – law – church polity – theology of law – solidarity – love and law – charity – justice – agape – caritas

1 Introduction

1.1 *Introduction, Question, and Composition*

On 10 December, two events are remembered, both of which are relevant to the subject of this book. These are the anniversary of the Universal Declaration of Human Rights and of the burning of canon law books and the papal bull by Martin Luther (1483–1546). Below, I elaborate on the relevance of these two events to the subject of this book. These concern the role of charity against the background of the notion of charity in law, theology of law, and church polity. The jurist's attention may immediately turn to the legal term *naasten*, from the Old Dutch word *naesten* or *vernaerderen*.[1] This refers to use 'of the right to take

1 Related designations in Dutch are: naastingrecht, naastbaar, vernaasten, vernaasting,

 | DOI:10.1163/9789004679979_002

the place of the purchaser in the sale of property'.[2] Sometimes it also refers to movable property.[3] It is also applied 'to making use of the right to repurchase by the seller' and 'to make use of the right to become the owner of something for a certain fee'.[4] In general, the verb neighbouring (*naasten*) now means 'to take possession'. This book, however, as already indicated, is about charity and the right of the neighbour or neighbourly law, even though the verb 'to neighbour' or a derivation thereof can also be included. Charity can be defined as 'love of one's neighbour'. Traditionally, this can refer to a relative, but it can also refer to the whole person or fellow human being.[5] The designation of the right of the neighbour refers to the right of the neighbour that is dialectically intertwined with the divine law and is an expression of man's solidarity with his fellow man. I borrow this from the German legal philosopher and church law scholar Erik Wolf (1902–1977), whom I introduce in more detail below and whose central notion of neighbour law I aim to elaborate there.

The guiding research question in my argument, introduced in this opening section, is what meaning charity, or neighbourly law, has or should have in civil law, philosophy of law, theology of law, and church law. Section 2 is about German theology of law, and *das Nächstenrecht*. Section 3 concerns the theme of love and law in the Anglo-Saxon world. Section 4 deals with the topic of legal philosophers on 'the other'. In section 5, the focus is drawn to the principle of reciprocity and legal objects in law. It is followed by section 6 on theology of law on 'the other'. It is followed by section 7 on church law and 'the other'. In section 7, I will not only point out to some relevant articles of church orders but also to other voices in denominations. So, it is not only about the ecclesial voice of religious leaders via church orders of relevant denominations, but also to consider how such a voice is echoed by the voice in practice. In this regard, it is also about the application of the voice of the church order with view to neighbourliness. In section 8, an answer to the central research question will be formulated.

---

naaster, naasting, ontnaasten, naastkoop; "Historische woordenboeken," accessed 24 September 2024, https://gtb.ivdnt.org.

2 Instituut voor de Nederlandse Taal, "Historische woordenboeken," accessed 24 September 2024, https://gtb.ivdnt.org.

3 Sybrandus J. Fockema Andreae, *Oud-Nederlandsch Burgelijk Recht* 2 (Haarlem: Bohn, [1906]), 267ff.

4 Instituut voor de Nederlandse Taal, "Historische woordenboeken," accessed 24 September 2024, https://gtb.ivdnt.org.

5 Ton den Boon, Dirk Geeraerts and Nicoline van der Sijs, *Van Dale Groot woordenboek van de Nederlandse taal* 2, 14th ed. (Utrecht/Antwerpen: Van Dale Lexicografie, 2005), 2242.

1.2 *The Right to Be Recognised as a Person*

As mentioned above, the day of my inaugural lecture was the 73rd anniversary of the Universal Declaration of Human Rights (UDHR). For the topic of neighbour law, the right of the person in relationship with the other person is relevant. This declaration maintains in article 6: 'Everyone, wherever he is, has the right to be recognised as a person before the law.'[6] 10 December 2023 was the 75th anniversary of this declaration. Every year, on December 10, the Netherlands Institute for Human Rights[7] travels to high schools across the Netherlands to show students the importance of human rights. This is important, given the geopolitical and domestic social context today, for example the war between Russia and the Ukraine, between Israel and the Palestinian territories, and the changed situation in Syria, and considering how important it is to keep in mind the context of the genesis of the Universal Declaration of Human Rights in 1948, shortly after the end of World War II. The Netherlands Institute for Human Rights considers that education on human rights is crucial. In general, this institute,

> publishes research, advises the government and parliament, reports to international human rights institutes, provides information and promotes human rights education. The Institute also reviews individual cases to determine whether someone has been discriminated against at work, at school or as a consumer. In addition, the Institute monitors the implementation of the UN Convention on the Rights of Persons with Disabilities in the Netherlands.

Where the freedom of millions of people was restricted, ignored, and worse, the UDHR was supposed to help safeguard people's rights. That annual remembrance of its genesis and relevance is important, was demonstrated by Minister of Justice and Security (2017–2022) Ferdinand B.J. Grapperhaus when, on 10 December 2018, he delivered the opening address of the congress organised by the Centre for Religion and Law, a partnership of the Faculty of Religion and Theology, and the Faculty of Law of the Vrije Universiteit Amsterdam, to mark the UDHR's 70th anniversary.[8]

---

6 United Nations, "Universal Declaration on Human Rights," accessed 24 September 2024, https://www.un.org/en/about-us/universal-declaration-of-human-rights.

7 In Dutch: het *College voor de Rechten van de Mens*; College voor de Rechten van de Mens, "Home," accessed 24 September 2024, https://www.mensenrechten.nl/.

8 In 2023 the Theological University Kampen | Utrecht became the third partner in the Centre for Religion and Law; Centrum voor Religie en Recht, "Centrum voor Religie en Recht," accessed https://www.mensenrechten.nl, https://www.religie-recht.nl/.

We need not limit ourselves to 10 December of each calendar year to have care and concern for the rights of others. Every day of the calendar year provides many opportunities to do so. This is especially true when fundamental rights are increasingly horizontal due to the clash of fundamental rights between citizens, since fundamental rights have traditionally been vertical rights requiring that the government should refrain from actions or statements against citizens. Increasingly, it is about standing up for someone's individual rights. This is necessary in cases where people's rights are trampled. Then individuals have the right to rise, raise their voices, and stand up for themselves. Yet in an individualistic era, this has taken on a one-sided emphasis. The trap is that the emphasis becomes more on 'my' rights and not those of the other(s). Not without reason, amid criticism of the UDHR, attention is drawn to human duties and the notion of human dignity.[9] This also needs to be put in the context of criticism of the UDHR. The UDHR should not be considered only from the perspective of human rights, but also from the dimension of human dignity. The main criticism is that this declaration is or might be Western, colonial, and Christian in nature.[10] That would mean that the declaration is not universal as it would not include the Global South perspective and a multiple perspective of religions and world views. From today's dimension one could also hold that the UDHR has an eye less on gender, climate change, and the rights of animals. Here is not the place to elaborate on this criticism.

1.3 *Book and Bull Burning*

10 December is an interesting and important day for another reason. On 10 December 1520, at the day of my inaugural lecture 501 years ago, Martin Luther burned the papal bull *Exsurge Domine* (Arise, O Lord)[11] along with some canon law books of the Roman Catholic Church.[12] The bull called on him to revoke

---

9 Cf. among others Pablo Gilabert, *Human Dignity and Human Rights* (Oxford: Oxford University Press, 2018); David Kretzmer and Ekhart Klein, eds., *The Concept of Human Dignity in Human Rights Discourse* (The Hague: Kluwer Law International, 2002).

10 Janne Mende, "Are human rights western – And why does it matter? A perspective from international political theory," *Journal of International Political Theory* 17, no. 1 (2019), accessed 14 June 2024, https://doi.org/10.1177/1755088219832992; A. Mayer, *Redefining rights: OIC attempts to reshape values in the* UN *human rights system*, in A.T. Chase, ed., *Routledge Handbook on Human Rights and the Middle East and North Africa* (London: Routledge: 2017), pp. 170–181; P.P. Karan, *The Non-western World: Environment, Development, and Human Rights* (New York: Taylor & Francis, 2005).

11 *Exsurge Domine* is taken from Psalm 10:12.

12 Cf. Sabine Hiebsch, "Luther en (kerk)recht: Een verkenning," in *Geest of Recht? Kerkrecht tussen ideaal en werkelijkheid*, eds. Leon van den Broeke and Hans Schaeffer (Kampen: Summum Academic Publications, 2019), 13 (*Deddens Kerkrecht Serie* 3, ed. Leon van den Broeke).

his statements within a 60-day period. On 10 December 1520, that deadline expired. Luther did not recant his views on the abuses in the Church of the time. The book and bull burning are used by Reformed people in the past and in the present to express their negative attitude towards and decline of everything which has to do with rules, law, and church order. This has negative implications for everything which has to do with church organisation and the law of and in the church. However, Luther and his disciples showed that they took the relationship between church and law seriously.[13] Then as well as today, it was about no less than freedom – not only of the community of faith, but also of the right of the individual in the community of faith and in society.[14] The notion of loving one's neighbour applies not only to communities of faith, but also to individuals.

1.4 *Seeking Justice*

Sometimes tensions in faith communities lead to court. Things can get adversarial, despite normative statements of faith in religious celebrations and the doctrines of faith and the ethical actions expected of faith communities towards their neighbours. There is then no longer trust in the internal justice of faith communities. The holy church is not perceived as a safe church.

Despite the Apostle Paul's concern about taking sometimes disputes 'before the ungodly for judgment instead of before the Lord's people' some adherents of faith communities sue their religious leaders, the board of their faith community or denomination or even fellow believers before court. Church members, ministers, church councils and religious leaders see that there is more justice *outside* the faith community to be obtained than *in* the faith community.[15]

---

13 Cf. for example Philip Melanchton, "*Opera Quae Supersunt* Omnia," in *Corpus Reformatorum* XXII (CR), ed. Heinrich Ernst Bindseil (Brunsvigae: apud C.A. Schwetschke et filium, 1855), 224, 610; CR 21:81, 229, 561; CR 22:47; Martin Chemnitz, *Loci theologici Dn. Martini Chemnitii, theologi …: qvibvs et Loci commvnes D. Philippi Melanchthonis perspicue explicantur, & quasi integrum Christianæ doctrinæ corpus, ecclesiæ Dei sinceré proponitur*, ed. Polycarpus Leyser (Francofvrti: Typis & sumptibus Ioannis Spiessij, 1604); Niels Hemmingsen, *De lege naturae apodictica methodus concinnata per Nicolaum Hemmingium* (Witebergae: excudebant Haeredes Georgij Rhau, 1562); Johannes Eisermann, *Jo. Ferrarii, Montani, adnotationes in IIII Institutionum Iustiniani libros* (Apud Marpurgum: [Fran. Rhodus excudebat], xiij kal. April. añ. xxxij [20 Mar. 1532]) and Johannes Oldendorp, *Wat byllich ist und recht: Die deutsche Erstlingsschrift des sogenannten Naturrechts* (Frankfurt/Main, Sauer & Auvermann, 1969, reprint of the ed. published in Rostock in 1529, introduction A. Freybe).

14 Martin Luther, *Von der Freiheit eines Christenmenschen = De libertate Christiana*, ed. Reinhold Rieger (Tübingen: Mohr Siebeck, 2007) (*Kommentare zu Schriften Luthers* 1).

15 Cf. 1 Corinthians 6:1–11.

There is also sometimes little or no trust by faith communities in the government or state law if there is a perception that it restricts religious freedom from and within the faith community. Then, one's own religious right is perceived as most important. In some jurisdictions around the world, legislation and constitutional changes have been proposed for voters to consider on the ballot in the elections currently under way that would guarantee the right to worship as deserving the highest legal scrutiny within the overarching framework of religious freedom. Restricting religious freedom to a right to worship is actually controversial in religious freedom circles for ignoring many ways churches minister and exercise their rights outside of the worship context, including through charitable and social work.[16] In international law, religious freedom rights have been fleshed out beyond the relatively brief statements in the UDHR and in the International Covenant on Civil and Political Rights (ICCPR)[17] in the 1981 UN Declaration on the Elimination of All Forms of Intolerance and of Discrimination Based on Religion or Belief, which lists many more dimensions of religious freedom than 'freedom of thought, conscience, and belief' or even a 'right to worship'.

Legal egoism lurks. By that designation, I mean that people are focused only on their own legal interest, making themselves central to the detriment of others. As a result, the focus in faith communities on the *causae miserabilium personarum* – the interests of the unprotected, biblically speaking the group of widows, orphans and the poor – can be undermined, whether in favour of the law of the church or not.[18] Churches limit themselves when the focus is on worship and not ministry to the vulnerable. With ministry, greater outreach is intended. Of course the *causa miserabilium personarum* was not always lim-

---

16 Cf. CBN News / Gary Lane, "Hillary Clinton, Progressives and the Freedom to Worship," accessed 16 May 2024, https://www1.cbn.com/globallane/archive/2016/11/11/hillary-clinton-progressives-and-the-freedom-to-worship; for the enhanced protections of the 1981 Declaration: John Witte Jr. and Michael Green, "Religious Freedom, Democracy, and International Human Rights," in *Rethinking Religion and World Affairs*, eds. Timothy Samuel Shah, Alfred Stephan, and Monica Duffy Toft (Oxford: Oxford University Press, 2012), 104–124.

17 United Nations Human Rights Office of the High Commissioner, "International Covenant on Civil and Political Rights," accessed 16 May 2024, https://www.ohchr.org/en/instruments-mechanisms/instruments/international-covenant-civil-and-political-rights.

18 Cf. Erik Wolf, *Ordnung der Kirche: Lehr- und Handbuch des Kirchenrechts auf ökumenischer Basis* (Frankfurt am Main: Vittorio Klostermann, 1961), 254; Willibald M. Plöchl, *Geschichte des Kirchenrechts*, 2nd ed. (Wien/München: Herold, 1960), I, 221–33; II, 305–29; Virpi Mäkinen, Jonathan William Robinson, Pamela Slotte, and Heikki Haara, eds., *Rights at the Margins: Historical, Legal and Philosophical Perspectives* (Leiden/Boston: Brill, 2020) (*Brill's Studies in Intellectual History* 316); Thomas Duve, *Studien zum ius singulare und den privilegia miserabilium personarum, senum und indorum in Alter und Neuer Welt* (Frankfurt am Main: Klostermann 2008) (*Studien zur europäischen Rechtsgeschichte* 231).

ited to the most vulnerable, for it also included 'soldiers, foreign merchants, pilgrims and strangers' as belonging to the group of 'wretched persons or unfortunate persons'.[19] Since the legislation and ordering of the twelfth-century canonical jurist Gratian,[20] these regulations, like those surrounding the notion of *pro bono*, came into canon law in such a way that *personae miserabiles* could assert their rights in ecclesiastical courts.[21] In this way, the church facilitated the care of persons in need of special legal protection.[22] The secular authorities adopted this form of legal protection. From the ecclesiastical context, the legal protection of vulnerable groups was a canonical manifestation of the biblical and therefore ecclesiastical mandate of charity. It is or should be inherent to the essence of the Christian faith community that it bases itself on the Bible with its works of mercy.[23] In other words, the Christian community of faith and its members cannot escape the command to love their neighbour as themselves.[24]

1.5 *Neighbour Law*

This command and legal egoism constitute the reason to call attention to the right of the individual and the collective, especially focusing on what German colleagues call *das Nächstenrecht* – the right of the neighbour. *Nächstenrecht* includes both the relative status, capabilities, responsibilities, and rights of the neighbour, and the right of a vulnerable neighbour. In a fragmented society, and doubly so in religious communities, it can surely do no harm to pay attention not only to the legal position and rights of the potentially charitable individual and the religious community, but also to the right of the vulnerable neighbour.

The neighbour, the Hebrew Bible (Old Testament) teaches, is not only the fellow Israelite, but also the non-Israelite, the stranger, ('love thy neighbour as

19 Griet Vermeersch, "'Miserabele personen' en hun toegang tot het stadsbestuur," *Low Countries Journal of Social and Economic History* 12, no. 4 (2015): 1–27.

20 Cf. Anders Winroth, *The making of Gratian's Decretum* (Cambridge: Cambridge University Press, 2000); cf. Universiteitsbibliotheek Gent, "Decretum Gratiani," accessed https://www.mensenrechten.nl, https://lib.ugent.be/en/catalog/rug01:000794409.

21 Cf. Vermeersch, "'Miserabele personen' en hun toegang tot het stadsbestuur," 2.

22 Cf. Plöchl, *Geschichte des Kirchenrechts* II, 456. In positive law, *personae miserabiles* are minors and *curandi*; Book 1:345 and Book 4:193 Civil Code; Ronald Brinkman en Ilsemarie Breemhaar, 'The acceptance on behalf of personae miserabiles of a making, to which charges or conditions are attached.' In Dutch: 'De aanvaarding namens personae miserabiles van een making, waaraan lasten of voorwaarden zijn verbonden'; *Weekblad voor Privaatrecht, Notariaat en Registratie* 7263 (2019): 886–893.

23 Matt. 25:31–46.

24 Lev. 19:18, Matt. 19:19, Matt. 22:39, Mk. 12:31, Rom. 13:9, Gal. 5:14, Jac. 2:8 ('het koninklijke gebod', the royal commandment).

thyself') וְאָהַבְתָּ֥ לְרֵעֲךָ֖.[25] The Hebrew word רֵעַ (*re'a*) can mean both friend or companion, a fellow (meaning a fellow citizen) and the other.[26] Leviticus 19 and the New Testament voices align with it: τὸν πλησίον (*plèsion*)[27] is the neighbour. In English, it can also be translated as the fellow man, e.g. Matthew 19:19.[28] Old Testament scholar Henk Jagersma (1927–2016), in his doctoral dissertation on Leviticus, mentioned that the role of entry liturgies 'shows that there is a basis in the Old Testament for a commandment like Leviticus 19:18 in the covenant spirit'.[29] With a view to entrance liturgies, Broyles refers to Psalms 15

---

25 Cf. Henk Jagersma, *"Leviticus 19": Identiteit, bevrijding, gemeenschap*, PhD diss. University Utrecht (Assen: Van Gorcum & Comp./H.J. Prakke & H.M.G. Prakke, [1972]).

26 Francis Brown, ed., *The New Brown–Driver–Briggs–Gesenius Hebrew and English Lexicon with an Appendix containing the biblical Armaic* (Peabody Massachusetts: Hendrickson), 1979, 945b–46a.

27 '*καὶ ἀγαπήσεις τὸν πλησίον σου ὡς σεαυτόν*' ('en heb uw naaste lief als uzelf', and love your neighbour as yourself); *Novum Testamentum Graece* (*Nestle-Aland*), 28 (Stuttgart: Deutsche Bibelgesellschaft, 2012), accessed 24 September 2024, https://www.academic-bible.com/en/online-bibles/novum-testamentum-graece-na-28/read-the-bible-text/bibel/text/lesen/stelle/50/190001/199999/ch/7946f9f7f5fcda8de294600d3307c3b8/.

28 Lev. 19:18 and 19:34; Jagersma, *"Leviticus"*, 98–102; *A Greek-English Lexicon of the New Testament and Other Early Christian Literature: A Translation and Adaption of the Fourth Revised and Augmented Edition of Walter Bauer's Griechisch-Deutsches Wörterbuch zu den Schriften des Neuen Testaments und der übrigen urchristlichen Literatur*, by William F. Arndt and F. Wilburg Gingrich, eds. F. Wilburg Gingrich and Frederick W. Danker, 2nd ed. (Chicago/London, The University of Chicago Press, 1979), 672–673; "*ὁ πλησίον der Nachste,*" in *Theologisches Begriffslexikon zum Neuen Testament*, eds. Lothar Coenen, Erich Beyreuther and Hans Bietenhard, 2nd ed. (Wuppertal: Theologischer Verlag Rolf Brockhaus, 1970), 149–151; Jeffrey A. Gibbs, *Matthew 11:2–20:34* (Saint Louis: Concordia Publishing House, 2010), 965 (*Concordia Commentary*); David L. Turner, *Matthew* (Grand Rapids MI: Baker Academic: 2008), 469 (*Baker Exegetical Commentary on the New Testament*); Nobuyoshi Kiuchi, *Leviticus* (Nottingham/Downers Grove, Illinois: Apollos/InterVarsity Press, 2007), 354–356 (*Apollos Old Testament Commentary* 3, eds. David W. Baker and Gordon J. Wenham); John W. Kleinig, *Leviticus* (Saint Louis: Concordia Publishing House, 2003), 409–417 (*Concordia Commentary: A Theological Exposition of Sacred Scripture*); Pierre Bonnard, *L'Évangile selon Saint Matthieu* (Neuchâtel: Delachaux & Niestlé, 1963), 288 (*Commentaire du Nouveau Testament* 1); W.H. Gispen, *Leviticus* (Kampen: Kok, 1950), 280–282 (*Commentaar op het Oude Testament*); David L. Turner, *Matthew* (Grand Rapids MI: Baker Academic: 2008), 469 (*Baker Exegetical Commentary on the New Testament*).

29 Jagersma refers to Isaiah 33:14–16; Ezechiel 18,5ff.; Psalm 15 and Psalm 24,4–6; Jagersma, *"Leviticus 19"*, 101–102. Cf. for entrance liturgies: Craig C. Broyles, 'Psalms Concerning the Liturgies of Temple Entry', in *The Books of Psalms: Composition and Reception*, eds. Peter W. Flint and Patrik D. Miller (Leiden/Boston: Brill, 2005), 248–287 (*VT Suppl Series* 99). In Dutch: 'Dit overzicht van de genoemde profeten en de intochtsliturgieën toont dat er in het Oude Testament een basis is voor een gebod als Leviticus 19,18 in de verbondsgedachte'; Jagersma, *"Leviticus 19"*, 102.

and 24 which scholars describe as entrance liturgies.[30] Such Torah-entrance psalms have, according to Day (1999:60) three principal parts.[31] First, they contain the 'question about who may be allowed access to' God's 'dwelling place'. Second, they include an answer, 'setting out the ethical requirements'. Third, they have 'word of blessing with regards to those who are qualified to enter' God's 'dwelling place'.[32]

There is, thus, an intertwinement between entrance liturgy in the Old Testament and law. It concerns 'justice and mercy'. These are the conditions to enter God's holy place of worship.[33] This has everything to do with the topic of this book: neighbour law. In this respect Broyles states:

> The one who enters the temple to seek Yahweh is one who does not maliciously slander others, nor commits evil against a friend, nor take up a reproach (illegitimately) against his/her neighbour (verse 3). The relational contexts of the term ער [neighbour, friend, companion] (Harris et al. 1980:2186) is well known especially in the psalms and in Sinai Covenant and Priestly Theology. The term refers to a fellow member of the covenant community (Ex 20:17; Lev 19:17–18) (Kessler 2013:401) and the statements requires that the true Yahweh's worshipper should not fabricate a reproach against his/her neighbour under no circumstance.[34]

Leviticus 19:34 indicates that such charity extends to the neighbour outside one's own people in Israel. We cannot ignore the central biblical notion of charity, nor the second part of the commandment of charity: to love oneself.[35] Following a response from a woman who wondered in despair how she could love another when she did not even love herself, Martin Buber (1878–1965) and Frans Rosenzweig (1886–1929) then translated the commandment slightly differently: 'Love your neighbour, he is like yourself.'[36]

---

30 Broyles, 'Psalms Concerning the Liturgies of Temple Entry', 135.

31 John Day, *Psalms*, (London: T&T Clark, 1999), 60.

32 Broyles, 'Psalms Concerning the Liturgies of Temple Entry', 137.

33 Broyles, 'Psalms Concerning the Liturgies of Temple Entry', 142.

34 Broyles, 'Psalms Concerning the Liturgies of Temple Entry', 140–141.

35 Cf. Herman Ridderbos, *De Komst van het Koninkrijk: Jezus' prediking volgens de synoptische evangeliën*, 3rd ed. (Kampen: Kok, 1985), 255–287; Pinchas Lapide, *Hoe heeft men zijn vijanden lief: Met een nieuwe vertaling van de Bergrede* (Kampen: Kok, 1984), 31–34.

36 In Dutch: 'Heb je naaste lief, hij is als jezelf'. Cf. Martin Buber and Frans Rosenzweig, *Die fünf Bücher der Weisung* (Köln/Olten: Hegner, 1954) (*Die Schrift*, verdeutscht von Martin Buber in Gemeinschaft mit Frans Rosenzweig 1), 31.

2 The Right of the Neighbour

2.1 *Foundations Drafts*

The biblical commandment to love one's neighbour is not only interesting for biblical scholars. In the research fields of law and church law this commandment has captured attention, especially in the German context. After the horrors of the Second World War, German theology of law flourished. Three jurists designed foundation systems of church law: state and church law scholar Johannes Heckel (1889–1963), legal philosopher and church law scholar Erik Wolf, and ecumenical church law scholar Hans Dombois (1907–1997).

In this section, I will focus mainly on Wolf, as he explicitly focused on neighbour law. In doing so, I do not want to shortchange the other two jurists. Hence a brief overview of Heckel and Dombois before I focus on Wolf. Heckel was concerned with the so-called *lex charitatis*, the law of *caritas* (*agapè*), the order of divine love.[37] In doing so, he was influenced by the study of and his interpretation of Luther and his views on the doctrine of the two realms: the realm of God and the realm of the world, that are not separate but distinct.[38] Unlike Augustine of Hippo (354–430), Luther was more positive about the realm of the world and of government. The two-kingdom doctrine is contextually important when it comes to Lutheran views on the relationship between church and state, between church law and state law, and on the position of church law and how that relationship between the notions of 'church' and 'law' should be understood. Heckel arrived at a dualistic understanding of canon law, namely that state law and canon law should be distinct. Dombois focused on the relationship between law and grace from an ecumenical-church law and liturgical-church law perspective, i.e., outside his own denominational tradition, in his hefty trilogy *Das Recht der Gnade*.[39]

---

37 Johannes Heckel, *Lex Charitatis: Eine juristische Untersuchung über das Recht in der Theologie Martin Luthers*, ed. Martin Heckel, 2nd ed. (Köln/Wien: Böhlau Verlag, 1973), 82f. and 134. German jurist and church law scholar Siegfried Grundmann (1916–1967) can be seen as a connecting figure. He connects Heckel's *lex charitatis* with Erik Wolf's *Recht des Nächsten* (1902–1977). Wolf, unlike Heckel who thought much more systematically, thinks dialectically.

38 Cf. Hiebsch, "Luther en (Kerk)Recht," 20.

39 Hans Dombois, *Das Recht der Gnade*, 3 vols. (Bielefeld: Luther-Verlag, 1961–1983).

2.2 *Neighbour Law*

Wolf had been working on the philosophy of law[40] since the interwar period, but he discovered that the philosophical foundation of law was inadequate in the light of the rise of the *Bekennende Kirche* (the Confessing Church) against the German state intervention in the church with the states' church (*Reichskirche*) and the states' bishop (*Reichsbisschof*). From 1933, Wolf and other German jurists with a fascination for theology and church law groped for theology of law.[41] Wolf's renewed teaching assignment and the foundation of a seminar for 'Rechtsphilosophie und Evangelisches Kirchenrecht' (Legal Philosophy and Evangelical-Lutheran Church Polity) at the university of Freiburg in Germany gave him an even greater opportunity to devote himself more intensively to church law from 1945 onwards. This seminar was the predecessor of the *Institut für Staatswissenschaft und Rechtsphilosophie* (Institute for Constitutional Science and Legal Philosophy).[42] In 1958, his *Recht des Nächsten: Ein rechtstheologischer Entwurf* on the right of the neighbour from a legal theological foundation perspective saw the light.[43]

Four centuries earlier, Luther had already considered neighbour law.[44] He saw natural law as the foundation of law, including contract law.[45] In that context, he called attention to debtors and especially to the poor.[46] Citing Luther's interpretation of the Magnificat, German theologian Martin Honecker (1934–2021) stated: 'The confession of the right is supposed to serve the benefit of the neighbour.'[47] Luther distinguished between 'winning justice

---

40 Cf. Erik Wolf, *Die Entwicklung des Rechtsbegriffs im reinen Naturrecht*, PhD diss. Jena, ([Jena: s.n.], 1924).

41 From 1936, Wolf became involved in the *Bekennende Kirche* although he did not openly fight the National Socialism, he had previously espoused. Only from late 1941 would he have become an opponent of National Socialism.

42 Universität Freiburg, "Über das Institut," accessed 29 January 2024, https://www.jura.uni-freiburg.de/de/institute/rphil/institut/ueber_das_institut?set_language=de.

43 Erik Wolf, *Recht des Nächsten: Ein Rechtstheologischer Entwurf* (Frankfurt am Main: Vittorio Klostermann, 1958) (*Philosophische Abhandlungen* XV).

44 WA 17, 102, 8–12; WA 6, 3–8; WA 6, 36–60; WA 15, 293–313; WA 51, 331–424.

45 WA 6Ti, 7013, 326; WA 6, 459, 26–29; WA 11, 280, 13–19.

46 Cf. Astorri, *Lutheran Theology*, 55.

47 In German: 'Das Bekenntnis des Rechts soll nähmlich dem Nutzen des Nächsten dienen (…)'; Martin Luther, "Das Magnificat verdeutschet und ausgelegt," (1521). In WA 7, 583, 15–16; Martin Honecker, "Recht, Ethos, Glaube," *Zeitschrift für evangelisches Kirchenrecht* 29 (1984), 393. Cf. for the *Magnificat* also the book of my *Doktorvater* Christoph Burger, *Marias Lied in Luthers Deutung: Der Kommentar zum Magnifikat (Lk 1, 46b–55) aus den Jahren 1520/21* (Tübingen: Mohr Siebeck, 2007) (*Spätmittelalter und Reformation. Neue Reihe* 34).

and confessing justice'.[48] If a person does not succeed in getting justice done, it does not absolve the person from the obligation to continue working for justice. This does not happen automatically. John Calvin (1509–1564) recognised the difficulty involved in 'that all the endowments which we possess are divine deposits entrusted to us for the very purpose of being distributed for the good of our neighbour' and '(...) we shall not only unite the study of our neighbour's advantage with a regard to our own, but make the latter subordinate to the former'.[49] A great jurist like Johannes Althusius (1563–1638) pointed out that once a party knowingly agrees to a contract, the other party tries or other parties try to get out from under the contractual obligations.[50] Yet a person should not seek his own benefit, but that of another and also the honour of God, because God is merciful and gracious.[51] Lutheran church historian Sabine Hiebsch, pointing to the contextuality of Luther's theology, stresses that in Luther's publication on the secular government or authority, the central point is 'that man does not live for himself but for his neighbour. In the service of his neighbour, it is also permissible for a Christian to perform tasks of the secular realm'.[52]

For Wolf, the relationship to one's neighbour was the foundation and centre of law.[53] His *Recht des Nächsten* was the written version of the speech he had delivered the previous year on the 500th anniversary of the University of Freiburg im Breisgau, Germany. He dedicated this publication to the Swiss systematic theologian Karl Barth (1886–1968), who started from the principle that

---

48 In German: 'Recht gewinnen und Recht bekennen'; Honecker, "Recht, Ethos, Glaube," 393; WA 7, 582, 19ff.

49 Institutes III.VII.5; John Calvin, *The Institutes of the Christian Religion*, transl. Henry Beveridge (Grand Rapids MI: Christian Classics Ethereal Library, 2002). Cf. Johannes Calvijn, *Institutie of onderwijzing in de christelijke godsdienst* 2, 3rd ed., transl. from Latin by A. Sizoo (Delft: W.D. Meinema, [1956]), 189.

50 Cf. Johannes Althusius, *Dicæologicæ libri tres: Totum & universum jus, quo utimur, methodicè complectentes: cum parallelis hujus & Judaici Juris tabulisq[ue] insertis atq[ue] indice triplici, uno, auctorum, altero, capitum singulorum & tertio, rerum & verborum locupletissimo & accuratissimo: opus tam theoriæ quàm praxeos aliarumq́ue facultatum studiosis utilissimum* (Prostant Francofurti: Apud Christophorum Corvinum, [MD]CXVIII), I.64–97 and II.11–22; cf. John Witte Jr., *The Reformation of Rights Law: Religion and Human Rights in Early Modern Calvinism* (Cambridge/New York: Cambridge University Press, 2007), 180.

51 'Misericordia (...) est de natura Dei (...)'; WA 42, 356, 22.

52 Martin Luther, "Von Weltlicher Obrigkeit, wie weit man ihr Gehorsam schuldig sei," (1523); WA 11, 245–281. In Dutch: 'dat de mens niet voor zichzelf maar voor zijn naaste leeft. In dienst van zijn naaste is het voor een christen ook geoorloofd taken van het wereldlijke rijk uit te oefenen'; Hiebsch, "Luther en (kerk)recht," 20–21; WA 39II, 39–91.

53 Cf. Wolf, *Recht des Nächsten*, 11.

church law is, among other things, *ius liturgicum*.[54] Liturgical law expresses the Christocratic fraternity gathered around the subject of congregational life: Jesus Christ, the Head of His church.[55] Barth had formulated the question:

> Is there a relationship between the reality of the sinner's justification, accomplished once and for all by God in Jesus Christ, through faith alone, and the problem of human right: an inner, a necessary, such a relationship by which, with divine justification, human right also becomes, in some sense, the object of Christian faith and responsibility, and thus also of Christian confession?[56]

Wolf tried to formulate an answer to this question. The foundation for Wolf's theology of law was the Word of God, in his legal framework what he called *biblische Weisung* – biblical instruction.[57] For him, this led to fraternal Christocracy and the Christocratic fellowship with an anthropology centred on Christ. The church is not governed by democracy or hierarchy, but by Christ. In doing so, he joined Barth's notions of Christocracy and fraternity.[58] In Christ, God has become man's neighbour.[59]

---

54 Karl Barth, *Die Ordnung der Gemeinde: Zur dogmatischen Grundlegung des Kirchenrechts*, München: Kaiser, 1955 / Karl Barth, *Kirchliche Dogmatik IV/ 2* (Zürich: Zollikon, 1955), 765–824.

55 Wilhelm Steinmüller writes about Wolf's legal philosophical context and development: 'In einem weiteren Punkt unterscheidet [Wolf, LvdB] er sich von Heckel: Wolfs 'christokratisch-bruderschaftliche' Rechtstheologie ist nicht zu verstehen ohne die Kenntnis seiner rechtsphilosophischen Entwicklung'; Wilhelm Steinmüller, *Evangelische Rechtstheologie: Zweireichelehre. Christokratie. Gnadenrecht* 1 (Köln/Graz: Böhlau Verlag, 1968), 258.

56 In German: 'Gibt es eine Beziehung zwischen der Wirklichkeit der von Gott in Jesus Christus ein für allemal vollzogenen Rechtfertigung des Sünders allein durch den Glauben und dem Problem des menschlichen Rechtes: eine innere, eine notwendige, eine solche Beziehung, durch die mit der göttlichen Rechtfertigung auch das menschliche Recht in irgendeinem Sinn zum Gegenstand des christlichen Glaubens und der christlichen Verantwortung und damit auch des christlichen Bekenntnisses wird'; Karl Barth, *Eine Schweizer Stimme*, 1938/45 (s.a.: Zollikon, 1945), 8.

57 Cf. Erik Wolf, *Ordnung der Kirche*, 24–25, 466–469; Erik Wolf, *Rechtsgedanke und biblische Weisung: Drei Vorträge* (Tübingen: Furche-Verlag, [1947]) (*Forschungen der Evangelischen Akademie* 5).

58 In German: the notions of *Christokratie* and *Bruderschaft*; Barth, *Die Ordnung der Gemeinde*, 765–824.

59 Cf. Wolf, *Das Recht des Nächsten*, 16; cf. Barth, *Die Ordnung der Gemeinde*, 36–37.

2.3 *Personality and Solidarity*

With Wolf, divine law and neighbourly law are developed into the law of love and anchored in the theological anthropology (theoanthropology) of law. Divine law and neighbourly law are dialectically united and deepened into the love law of Christocracy and fraternity in the ecclesial context – not as suggestive of Christian nationalism, Christian politics or whatsoever. The analogy of divine law and neighbourly law leads to these two theological dimensions of law: personality and solidarity.[60] The vertical-horizontal personality in solidarity is the order of love and order of grace.[61] Whoever 'personally' respects the divine law, responds to the voice of God and answers to God, exercises solidary neighbourly law, Wolf argued. The two theological dimensions of law together form the Constitution of Christocracy, God's right to rule over us, and community.[62] Where God's right to rule looks at the order of Christocracy, the service law to the neighbour looks at the order of the fraternity.[63] Law and love are dialectically one. Love without law is disordered love; law without love is loveless. Love makes law into law and law orders love into *ordo caritatis*, the rule of charity. The church's legal order is a paradoxical order because it is based on the biblical instruction and also concretely represents a human order 'is proven and concretely a human order'.[64] It is an ordering of a community of sinful and redeemed people at the same time. The divine law is no longer just absolute law '*on* the human being, but also right *for* him'.[65] For Wolf, the right of the neighbour is as divine law the primal right of all fundamental rights.[66]

In his ecumenical disposition, Wolf always sought the common. In his view, it was sacred to recognize unity in diversity. German church law scholar, mathematician, and psychotherapist Wilhelm Steinmüller (1934–2013) thought that Wolf thought and lived from the perspective of the wholeness of life. In it, Wolf did not brush away the paradox of people and the church in the '"At the same time" of secular and spiritual, of holy and sinful, of visible and invisible, of universal and particular, of past and present'.[67] On the contrary, for Wolf, that

---

60 Wolf, *Das Recht des Nächsten*, 16–17.

61 In German: "'Ordnung der Liebe' und 'Ordnung der Gnade'"; Steinmüller, *Evangelische Rechtstheologie* 1, 407–413.

62 Wolf, *Das Recht des Nächsten*, 16–17.

63 Wolf, *Das Recht des Nächsten*, 16–17.

64 In German: 'erwiesen ist und konkret eine menschliche Ordnung'; Wolf, *Ordnung der Kirche* 6, 193. See also his: *Rechtstheologische Studien*, ed. Alexander Hollerbach (Frankfurt am Main: Klostermann, 1972).

65 In German: '*am* Menschen, sondern auch Recht *für* ihn'; Steinmüller, *Evangelische Rechtstheologie* 1, 405.

66 Wolf, *Recht des Nächsten*, 16.

67 In German: '"Zugleich" von weltlich und geistlich, von heilig und sündig, von sichtbar und unsichtbar, von universal und partikular, von vergangen und gegenwärtig hinein-

antithesis was in the context of following Christ and focusing on neighbour. Church law was thus not seen in a narrow sense as the law of a private church, not even so much the law that applies in a church, but as a function of Christian existence.

2.4 *Parable of the Workers in the Vineyard*

The right of the neighbour continued to preoccupy Wolf. On the 400th anniversary of the Heidelberg Catechism in 1963, he delivered a speech on *Ordnung der Liebe*.[68] A year later, he concentrated once more on the right of the neighbour in his publication *Gottesrecht und Nächstenrecht*. He did so use the parable of the workers in the vineyard from the Gospel according to Matthew 20:1–6.[69] The first-hour workers take issue with the vineyard owner's decision to give the workers who started later the same salary as those who worked from early in the morning. Wolf's point was to show that the guiding principles of a biblical theology of justice should not be interpreted as prescriptive law. They do not have a normative but a guiding or orienting function, 'a twofold guiding significance.'[70] On the one hand, they circumscribe any claim to justice on the part of human beings when it comes to manoeuvring the law to their own advantage, or to their disadvantage of others. On the other hand, these guiding principles justify 'the divine mandate of man to give his neighbour his right, to let him have his right and thus to remain in the right before God'.[71] In this way, Wolf argued, 'Biblical instruction becomes the guideline for a social existence that corresponds to the revealed will of God: the order of love in God's commandment and neighbourly law'.[72]

spannt'; Alexander Hollerbach, "In memoriam Erik Wolf †," *Zeitschrift der Savigny-Stiftung für Rechtsgeschichte/Kanonistische Abteilung* 65 (1979): 460.

68 Erik Wolf, *Ordnung der Liebe: Gottesgebot und Nächstenrecht im Heidelberger Katechismus* [*Votrag zur 400-Jahr-Feier des Heidelberger-Katechismus*] (Frankfurt/Main: Klostermann, 1963).

69 Erik Wolf, *Gottesrecht und Nächstenrecht: Rechtstheologische Exegese des Gleichnisses von den Arbeitern im Weinberg* (*Mt. 20:1–6*), s.l.: s.n., [1964]. Special print from: *Gott in Welt, Festgabe für Karl Kahner zum 60. Geburtstag am 5. März 1964*, eds. Johannes Baptist Metz et. al., vol. 2, Freiburg/Basel/Wien: Herder, 1964, 640–662.

70 In German: 'eine zwiefach wegleitende Bedeutung'; Wolf, *Gottesrecht und Nächstenrecht*, 641.

71 In German: 'den göttlichen Auftrag des Menschen, dem Nächsten sein Recht zu geben, ihn in seinem Recht zu lassen und damit vor Gott im Recht zu bleiben'; Wolf, *Gottesrecht und Nächstenrecht*, 641.

72 In German: 'wird Biblische Weisung zur Richtschnur eines sozialen Daseins, das dem offenbarten Gotteswillen: der Ordnung der Liebe in Gottesgebot und Nächstenrecht, entspricht'; Wolf, *Gottesrecht und Nächstenrecht*, 642.

From Wolf's aforementioned publications, the picture emerges that for him the right of love is the right of the neighbour.[73] The relationship between work and employer is the existential relationship with God.[74] To God's question, man answers. From this answer follows responsibility. This Wolf referred to as personality.[75] From the divine law follows the human law in the manner of neighbour's right, at least that is how Wolf understood the parable.[76] No one may make the other a neighbour. No one may claim what is due to the other as his or her right.[77] What is divinely ordained is, when it comes to the neighbour's right, binding.[78]

2.5 *Criticism on the Foundation Drafts around Neighbour Law*

The three foundation drafts around neighbour law of Heckel, Wolf and Dombois did not go unmentioned. According to Hans-Richard Reuter, the three great legal theological and ecclesiastical drafts of the theologically minded jurists Wolf (*Recht des Nächsten*, the right of the neighbour), Heckel (*lex charitatis*, charity law) and Dombois (*Recht der Gnade*, the right of grace) were methodically unsustainable. Reuter states: 'The spiritualisation of law in Johannes Heckel, the ontologisation of legal relationships in Erik Wolf and the juridification of spiritual action in Hans Dombois are different expressions of a theologising exaltation of law, which strives not to place the law "one floor too low"'.[79]

When it comes to Wolf's notion of neighbour's right, Reuter considers it problematic as the centre and foundation of church law. He also finds Wolf's foundational design a theological exaggeration of law, as if interpersonal law

73 Wolf, *Ordnung der Kirche*, 515.

74 Wolf, *Ordnung der Kirche*, 515.

75 Wolf, *Gottesrecht und Nächstenrecht*, 642.

76 Wolf, *Gottesrecht und Nächstenrecht*, 642.

77 Cf. Wolf, *Gottesrecht und Nächstenrecht*, 659.

78 Wolf, *Gottesrecht und Nächstenrecht*, 645.

79 In German: 'Die Spiritualisierung des Rechts bei Johannes Heckel, die Ontologisierung von Rechtsverhältnissen bei Erik Wolf und die Juridifizierung geistlichen Handelns bei Hans Dombois sind unterschiedliche Ausprägungen einer theologisierenden Überhöhung des Rechts, die bestrebt ist, das Recht nur ja nicht "ein Stockwerk zu tief" anzusetzen'; Hans-Richter Reuter, "Der Rechtsbegriff des Kirchenrechts in systematisch-theologischer Sicht," in *Das Recht der Kirche: Band 1 Zur Theorie des Kirchenrechts*. ed. Gerhard Rau, Hans-Richard Reuter en Klaus Schlaich (Gütersloh: Chr. Kaiser Gütersloher Verlagshaus, 1997), 236–286 (*Forschungen und Berichte der Evangelischen Studiengemeinschaft. Im Auftrag des Wissenschaftlichen Kuratoriums* 49, ed. Heinz Wismann). Previously Alwast Jendri researched Wolf's dialectics and theology of law in his *Dialektik und Rechtstheologie: Eine Grundlagenuntersuchung zu Ansatz und Methode der rechtstheologischen Konstruktion "Christokratie und Bruderschaft" von Erik Wolf* (Köln/Wien: Böhlau, 1985).

can be derived from 'legal elements of the relationship with God.'[80] It is stuck with Reuter on the cardinal question of the relationship between the notions of 'church' and 'law'. The relationship between those notions goes back to Luther and to the German legal historian and church law scholar Rudolf Sohm (1841–1917). His is the well-known twofold thesis: 'The nature of church polity is in conflict with the nature of the Church'.[81] After all, 'The nature of the church is spiritual, the nature of law is secular'.[82] For Sohm, the New Testament congregation was without any formal or legal organisation but was a charismatic entity, animated by the power of love, the primal model of all faith communities. For Sohm, the time-honoured adage applied: *ubi Christus, ibi ecclesia*, where Christ is, there is the church. This primordial model was replaced by the *Rechtskirche* – legal church – at the end of the first century AD. The adage was adapted: *ubi episcopus, ibi ecclesia*, where the bishop is, there is the church. Sohm therefore concluded that while the church of primordial Christianity was a purely spiritual church, the Roman Catholic Church was a spiritual-worldly church and the Evangelical Lutheran Church was a purely secular organisation from a legal perspective.[83] He therefore placed the *Geistkirche* or *Liebeskirche* – the spiritual or love church – and the *Rechtskirche* diametrically and incompatibly opposed to each other. The consequence of this was to leave the legal church for what it was. Having no affinity with the law of and in the church, perhaps even an aversion to it, is not foreign to Reformed church affiliations either.

Sohm's thesis has been the subject of much debate in the field. The discourse on this took a different turn with the German church struggle in the 1930s and 1940s. The *Bekennende Kirche* placed itself diametrically opposed to Sohm. The understanding of the *Bekennende Kirche* was that the order in and of the church should not be left to the government, but rather needed theological and confessional reflection and foundation. This was also expressed in the *Barmer Thesen*, the Barmen Declaration, specifically in theses 3 and 5 on the relationship between government and religion. More specifically, church law is Christocratically determined. Christ is the Head and Lord, the primary subject, of His church – the secondary subject. Dietrich Bonhoeffer (1909–1945)

80 In German: 'rechtlichen Elementen des Gottesverhältnisses'; Reuter, "Der Rechtsbegriff des Kirchenrechts in systematisch-theologischer Sicht," 267.

81 In German: 'Das Wesen des Kirchenrechtes steht mit dem Wesen der Kirche in Widerspruch'; Rudolph Sohm, *Kirchenrecht I: Die historische Grundlagen* (Leipzig: Verlag von Duncker & Humblot, 1892), 700.

82 In German: 'Das Wesen der Kirche ist geistlich, das Wesen des Rechtes ist weltlich'; Sohm, *Kirchenrecht* I, 700.

83 Cf. Sohm, *Kirchenrecht* I, 698.

went a step further in that Christ is not only the Head of the church, but also of the world.[84] In doing so, Bonhoeffer took a stand against the overemphasis on the realm of the sword, the government.

For Reuter, the question was whether in canon law, in the connection between the two heterogeneous notions of 'church' and of 'law', a comprehensive church concept and a double legal concept (law and order) has entered into the equation.[85] Reuter maintains this instead of the connection of a double church concept and a comprehensive legal concept as with Sohm, conversely with the Barmen Declaration. Reuter does not make it noticeably clear what exactly he means by this double church concept. He relies on the German systematic theologian and church and dogmatic historian Ernst Wolf (1902–1971). The latter makes it clear that it concerns the double church concept of the *ecclesia spiritualis* (spiritual church) and the *ecclesiae particulares* (private churches), or the *ecclesia invisibilis* (invisible church) and the *ecclesia visibilis* (visible church).[86] It ties in with Sohm's irreconcilable distinction between the spiritual church and the legal church.

Reuter did refer to the Barmen Declaration, which formed a theological and confessional protest against the *Deutsche Christen* (German Christians), an influential National Socialist movement in German Protestantism.[87] The Barmen Declaration assumed a comprehensive concept of church, but also a dual concept of law: law and of the more limited notion of order.[88] The Barmen Declaration seems to be more about order than law, but since the nature of the text is confessional, it did not elaborate on the question how to define a legal

84 Cf. Leon van den Broeke, "'Fear God, Honour the Emperor': The Barmen Declaration and its Reception in the Netherlands," in George Harinck and Hans-Georg Ulrichs, eds., *Naaste verwanten/Nahe Verwandte: Het gereformeerde protestantisme in Nederland en Duitsland in de twintigste eeuw/Der reformierte Protestantismus in den Niederlanden und in Deutschland im 20. Jahrhundert* (Amersfoort: De Vuurbaak, 2020), 161–89. (*ADChartasreeks* 36); Christine-Ruth Müller, *Bekenntnis und Bekennen: Dietrich Bonhoeffer in Bethel (1933). Ein lutherischer Versuch* (München: Chr. Kaiser, 1989).

85 Reuter, "Der Rechtsbegriff," 238; Ernst Wolf, "Sinn und Grenze der Anwendung der Zwei-Reiche-Lehre auf das Kirchenrecht," in *Staatsverfassung und Kirchenordnung: Festgabe für Rudolf Smend zum 80. Geburtstag am 15. Januar 1962*, eds. K. Hesse, S. Reicke and U. Scheuner (Tübingen: Mohr, 1962), 443–444; Cf. Johannes Heckel, *Das blinde, undeutliche Wort 'Kirche': Gesammelte Aufsätze*, ed. Siegfried Grundmann (Köln/Graz: Böhlau Verlag, 1964); Ernst Wolf, "Der christliche Glaube und das Recht: Zu J. Heckel, Lex charitatis," *Zeitschrift für evangelisches Kirchenrecht* 4 (1955): 225–253.

86 Wolf, "Sinn und Grenze der Anwendung der Zwei-Reiche-Lehre auf das Kirchenrecht," 444.

87 Cf. Eberhard Busch, *Die Barmer Thesen 1934–2004* (Göttingen: Vandenhoeck und Ruprecht, 2004).

88 Cf. Reuter, "Der Rechtsbegriff," 238.

concept compatible with the ecclesiastical order. Dutch historian George Harinck concluded in his inaugural address in 2003 that the Barmen Declaration was more a theological, confessional and apolitical statement than a resistance document with far-reaching social and political consequences against national socialism.[89] The Barmen Declaration sought to show the way amid the theological confusion and ecclesiastical disorder that the *Deutsche Christen* had caused. The Barmen Declaration constituted no more and no less than an internal church document. Harinck argues that the 'historian describes how it was, the theologian how it should be'.[90] The (church) lawyer and the legal theologian are concerned with both the *ius constitutum*, the law in force, and the *ius constituendum*, the law as it should be, also from the awareness that the law in force is imperfect and law continues to evolve.[91] Theologically formulated: Church law is also eschatological law.

In addition, Reuter considered the drafts problematic from the perspective of their application. He wondered to what extent it made sense to consider, for example, church disciplinary law and travel expenses as the right of love.[92] He therefore agreed with Eckhard Lessing (1935–2020): '"The magic of the close connection between theology and canon law has" long since "disappeared"'.[93] The downside of this is that there is no longer any relationship between theology and church law, and church law can be left to lawyers and encyclopaedically

89 George Harinck, *Tussen Barmen en Amsterdam: Rede uitgesproken op vrijdag 6 juni 2003 in de Burgwalkerk te Kampen bij de aanvaarding van het ambt van bijzonder hoogleraar namens het Archief- en Documentatiecentrum in de geschiedenis van de Gereformeerde Kerken in de context van het Nederlands protestantisme aan de Theologische Universiteit van de Gereformeerde Kerken in Nederland* (Amstelveen: EON Pers, 2003); Van den Broeke, "Fear God, Honour the Emperor," 161–189.

90 Harinck, *Tussen Barmen en Amsterdam*, 18.

91 Cf. Leon van den Broeke, "Het recht volgt het leven? Van wetboek en kerkorde naar kunstwerk en liedboek," in *Geest of Recht? Kerkrecht tussen ideaal en werkelijkheid*, ed. Leon van den Broeke and Hans Schaeffer (Kampen: Summum Academic Publications, 2019), 95–112 (*Deddens Kerkrecht Serie* 3, ed. Leon van den Broeke); Barth, *Die Ordnung der Gemeinde*; Gustav Heinemann, "Im Reiches dieses Königs hat man das Recht lieb (Ps. 99,4)," in *Glaubensfreiheit – Bürgerfreiheit. Reden und Aufsätze Kirche – Staat – Gesellschaft 1945–1975*, ed. Gustav W. Heinemann, 2nd ed., ed. Diether Koch, München: Chr. Kaiser, 1990, 124–32 / *Die Stimme der Gemeinde* 6 (1954): 385.

92 Reuter, "Der Rechtsbegriff," 238. In this way Reuter tried to apply abstract notions like eschatological law, and love and law, to the way the church deals with pragmatic aspects like the imbursement of travel expenses.

93 In German: 'Langst ist "der Zauber, der von der engen Verbindung von Theologie und Kirchenrecht ausgeht, gewichen"'; Reuter, "Der Rechtsbegriff," 239; Eckhard Lessing, "Das Verständnis der Ökumene im deutschen evangelischen Kirchenrecht nach dem 2. Weltkrieg," in *Kirche-Recht-Ökumene. Studien zur Ekklesiologie*, ed. Eckhard Lessing (Bielefeld: Luther-Verlag, 1982), 151.

in the legal education curriculum. To reassure lawyers: neither can church law be left to theologians alone, mindful of the words civil law scholar and senator Anne Anema (1872–1966) who once spoke, 'Church law, much church, little law.'[94] As much as Reuter's remark makes sense in terms of church law, it is questionable whether church disciplinary law and regulations on travel reimbursement cannot be considered an expression of neighbourly law.

Reuter is not alone in his criticism. Michael Welker joins him when he talks about the right of love in general, and problematicises the right of the neighbour:[95]

> The talk of the "right of love" mixes legal-theological and pneumatological forms and contents instead of clearly assigning them to each other. The phrase "right of the neighbour" erases the fruitful tension between legal and compassion-legal provisions, which in any case is of significant importance for the formation of the occidental ethos (and the moral communication shaped by this ethos).[96]

To illustrate, over a decade earlier, in 1984, Martin Honecker had denied the immediate legal relevance of concrete references to charity. He criticised Wolf's theology of law and his foundational design specifically focused on neighbourly law.[97] He also did not fully go along with systematic theologian Wolfhart Pannenberg (1928–2014). While he did agree with Pannenberg when it came to the cultural anthropological question of the relationship between law and religion, he could not go along with Pannenberg's alignment with

94 In Dutch: 'Kerkrecht, veel kerk, weinig recht'; H. Algra in *Leeuwarder Kerkbode*, acquired by K. Schilder, "Persschouw," *De Reformatie* 19, no. 6 (11 November 1938): 47–48. Also Piet Deddens refers to this comment made by Anema and elaborates on this in his twofold article in *De Reformatie*: "Kerkrecht: Veel kerk en weinig recht? I," *De Reformatie* 26, no. 1 (7 October 1950), 17; "Kerkrecht: Veel kerk en weinig recht? II," *De Reformatie* 26, no. 2 (14 October 1950): 28–30.

95 Michael Welker, "Recht in den biblischen Überlieferungen in systematisch-theologischer Sicht," in *Das Recht der Kirche*, 3 vols., eds. Gerhard Rau, Hans-Richard Reuter and Klaus Schlaich (Gütersloh: Chr. Kaiser/Gütersloher Verlagshaus, 1994–1997), 390 (*Forschungen und Berichte der Evangelischen Sudiengemeinschaft* 49–51, im Auftrag des Wissenschaftlichen Kuratoriums, ed. Heinz Wismann).

96 In German: 'Die Rede vom "Liebesrecht" vermischt gesetzestheologische und pneumatologische Formen und Inhalte, statt sie klar einander zuzuordnen. Die Wendung "Recht des Nächsten" tilgt die fruchtbare Spannung zwischen rechtlichen und erbarmensgesetzlichen Bestimmungen, die jedenfalls von großer Bedeutung für die abendländische Ethosbildung (und die von diesem Ethos geprägte moralische Kommunikation) ist'; Welker, "Recht in den biblischen Überlieferungen in systematisch-theologischer Sicht," 390.

97 Honecker, "Recht, Ethos, Glaube," 383–405.

Wolf's theological legal basis through the adage 'right through love'.[98] Despite Honecker's view that legal norms do not coincide with moral norms, he nevertheless argued that law has to do with the regulation of social relations while respecting the right of the individual.[99]

In German theology of law, and church polity discourse, the foundational designs of Wolf, Heckel and Dombois became nearly passé. Though, in the 1990s there was a revival by the 'Kommission Kirchenrecht – Evangelische Theologie' of the curatorium of the 'Evangelischen Studiengemeinschaft' that resulted in a three-volume work.[100] However, attention in the German-speaking profession to neighbour law as a basic design for church law disappeared. This affected not only Wolf's work but also the foundation designs of Heckel and Dombois.

3 Love and Law

Amidst these debates academic attention to the relationship between love and law had not completely disappeared. On the contrary, in Anglo-Saxon areas, more attention came to the research area of love and law. Centuries earlier, attention had been paid to contract law in relation to covenant theology. At the Theological University Kampen, where Klaas Schilder (1890–1952) ensured that covenant theology became a central notion in the Reformed Churches liberated, this must caught the imagination.[101] One can think of the German Lutheran theologian and philosopher Johann Franz Buddeus (1667–1729) who, in 1711 on the relationship between contract law and covenant theology, argued that equivalence between parties in contract law not only has a legal foundation but is rooted in and is an expression of Christian grace or mercy. One party helps improve, or at least not worsen, the position of the other party.[102]

---

98 Honecker, "Recht, Ethos, Glaube," 404.

99 Honecker, "Recht, Ethos, Glaube," 385.

100 Gerhard Rau, Hans-Richard Reuter and Klaus Schlaich, eds., *Das Recht der Kirche*, 3 vols. (Gütersloh: Chr. Kaiser/Gütersloher Verlagshaus, 1994–1997) (*Forschungen und Berichte der Evangelischen Sudiengemeinschaft* 49–51, im Auftrag des Wissenschaftlichen Kuratoriums, ed. Heinz Wismann).

101 Cf. a.o. K. Schilder, "Kerkverband en kerkverbond," in *Verzamelde werken 1944–1945*, ed. K. Schilder, bezorgd door G. Harinck and W.G. de Vries (Barneveld: De Vuurbaak, 2001), 17–35.

102 Astorri, *Lutheran Theology*, 166; Johann Franz Buddeus, *Institutiones theologiae moralis variis obseruationaibus illustratae*, (Lipsiae: apud Haeredes Thomae Fritsch, 1727), 544. Harold J. Berman points out that the nineteenth-century jurists were different from their predecessors. For him, the most striking difference was that they dissociated general contract law from its anchoring into religious, more specifically: to Christian doctrine of faith Berman; Berman, "The Christian sources of general contract law," in *Christianity and Law:*

American jurist Harold J. Berman (1918–2007) pointed to new developments. Nineteenth-century jurists were different from their predecessors.[103] It should be borne in mind that European contract law dates to the late eleventh or early twelfth century, respectively. Around 1200, canonists developed the general theory of contractual liability.[104] This held that a *nudum pactum*, a bare non-binding agreement, could give rise to a civil action.[105] Breaking a contract was considered a sin. It also protected the rights of the promised, the other contracting party. For Berman, the most striking difference was that nineteenth-century jurists began to detach general contract law from its anchoring in religious, more specifically Christian, doctrine and connected it to their own belief system 'based on rationalism and individualism' with freedom of the will and autonomy of parties as fundamental principles.[106] Berman states: 'Our contract law started (…) from the theory that a promise created an obligation to God, and that for the salvation of souls God instituted the ecclesiastical and secular courts with the task, in part, of enforcing contractual obligations to the extent that such obligations are just.'[107]

Berman's views are drawn from the conference volume that is the product of the conference on 'Love and Law' organised by Pepperdine University in Malibu, California US.[108] In this volume, editors Robert F. Cochran Jr. and Zachary R. Calo and a group of authors, including Berman, focus on how Christian love shapes law.[109] That love involves ἀγάπη (agape, charity). In addition, there are other meanings of the word love: ἔρως (*eros*, lust, erotic love), φιλία (*philia*, friendship) and στοργή (*storge*, instinctive love) – the love between parents and children and that between special friends.[110] The Dutch

---

An Introduction, eds. John Witte Jr. and Frank S. Alexander (Cambridge: Cambridge University Press, 2008), 127. Cf. for Islamic contract law: Valentino Cattelan, *Religion and Contract Law in Islam. From Medieval Trade to Global Finance* (Abingdon, Oxon/New York: Routledge, 2024) (*ICLARS Series on Law and Religion*).

103 Cf. Berman, "The Christian Sources of General Contract Law," 127.

104 Cf. Berman, "The Christian Sources of General Contract Law," 130.

105 Cf. Berman, "The Christian Sources of General Contract Law," 130; N.E. Algra and H.R.W. Gokkel, "Pactum," in *Fockema Andreae's verwijzend & verklarend juridisch woordenboek*, eds. N.E. Algra and H.R.W. Gokkel, 12th ed. (Groningen: Martinus Nijhoff, 2001), 356.

106 Berman, "The Christian Sources of General Contract Law," 127.

107 Berman, "The Christian Sources of General Contract Law," 132.

108 Pepperdine | Caruso School of Law, "Love and Law," accessed 24 September 2024, https://law.pepperdine.edu/nootbaar-institute/annual-conference/loveandlaw.

109 Robert F. Cochran, Jr and Zachary R. Calo, eds. *Agape, Justice and Law: How Might Christian Love Shape Law?* (Cambridge: Cambridge University Press, 2017) (*Cambridge Studies in Law and Christianity* ed. John Witte Jr).

110 Thomas Jay Oord, *The Nature of Love: A Theology* (St. Louis MO: Chalice Press, 2010); "ἀγάπη," in Bauer, *A Greek-English Lexicon of the New Testament*, ed. Arndt/Gingrich, 5–6; "Liebe," in *Theologisches Begriffslexikon zum Neuen Testament* 2, 895–906.

scholar of dogmatic theology Jan Veenhof explains in his book *Geist und Liebe* that agape reveals itself as a personal closeness, as a redeeming power.[111] Through agape, a person tries to do justice to another person, to contribute to the improvement of the other person's position, to interpret the voice of the other person, to bring redemption to another person who is stuck, to empower the other person.

In his comprehensive work, American philosopher Nicholas Wolterstorff not only relates the notions of love and law to the notion of justice, but also roots them in liturgy.[112] Love is not only a concept to theologise it in an abstract way, but also to concretise in law and justice in both the public domain and in (the *ius liturgicum* of) faith communities. In his *Hearing the Call*, for example, he connects not only liturgy and justice, but also church and world: 'Worship acceptable to God, authentic worship, is the worship of a pure heart. And the only pure heart is the heart of a person who has genuinely struggled to embody God's justice and righteousness in the world and genuinely repented of ever again doing so only halfheartedly.'[113] The latter seems to be kicking in an open (church) door. Yet this connection between church and world, between liturgy and justice, falters, while agape as a mission is inextricably intertwined with the Christian community of faith and its affiliates.

4 *Amor mundi* and the Other

4.1 Amor mundi

It is not only Christian lawyers or theologians who engage in reflection on and application of the notion of agape, or charity. Attention to 'the other'

---

111 Jan Veenhof, *Geist und Liebe: Die systematischen Voraussetzungen der Ethik Hendrik van Oyens* (Amsterdam: Rodopi, 1978), 49.

112 Cf. Nicholas Wolterstorff, *Hearing the Call: Liturgy, Justice, Church, and World*, ed. Mark R. Gornik en Gregory Thompson) (Grand Rapids MI / Cambridge UK: Wm.B. Eerdmans, 2011); Nicholas Wolterstorff, *Justice in Love* (Grand Rapids MI / Cambridge UK: Wm.B. Eerdmans, 2011); Nicholas Wolterstorff, *Justice: Rights and Wrongs* (Princeton: Princeton University Press, 2008); Nicholas Wolterstorff, *Until Justice and Peace Embrace: The Kuyper lectures for 1981 delivered at the Free University of Amsterdam* (Grand Rapids, Mich.: W.B. Eerdmans Pub. Co., 1983); Nicholas Wolterstorff, *Until Justice and Peace Embrace*, 2nd ed. (Grand Rapids: Eerdmans, 1994).

113 For example, his chapters "Justice as a Condition of Authentic Liturgy," and "Liturgy, Justice, and Holiness," Nicholas Wolterstorff, *Hearing the Call: Liturgy, Justice, Church and World*, eds. Mark R. Gornik en Gregory Thompson (Grand Rapids MI / Cambridge UK: Wm.B. Eerdmans, 2011), 39–58 resp. 59–79.

may be expected from a theological, ecclesiastical, and spiritual perspective, but good words are not enough. This was, among others, the reproach of the German American Jewish political philosopher Hannah Arendt (1906–1975). She posited that Christianity lacks a sincere *amor mundi* – the love for the world that encourages people to respect and care for it.[114] That includes the inhabitants of the world. Hence, this section from a (legal) philosophical perspective on love for the world, charity and the other.

Arendt's stance regarding Christianity and the lack of the love for the world can be understood. Unfortunately, Christianity has demonstrated not only its best practices but also its shadow sides – and it still does. However, one could state this about every religion. Moreover, one should also pay attention to the blind spots in one's religion. Is it really Christianity itself which lacks a sincere love for the world, or is it the religious leaders and/or (people in) faith communities who neglect the notion of this kind of love?

4.2 *The Face of the Other*

Love for the world is something that human beings cannot escape, as if by shaking off their own shadow. This *amor mundi* is unavoidable when one looks in the face of the other. The French-Jewish philosopher with Lithuanian roots, Emmanuel Levinas (1906–1995) showed penetratingly that the face of the other reflects us, even if the person is 'locked in' his or her 'own portrait', as it were.[115] According to Levinas, a person cannot be understood without speaking to him or her: 'I not only think he is, but I speak to him.'[116] To emphasise this, he frequently capitalised the Other (l'Autre). By doing so, he emphasised the unforgiving otherness of the defenceless other human being. The Other appeals to our responsibility. Levinas thus criticised both egology – the centrality of the 'I' – and the ontology in which the 'I' disappears into the all-encompassing and also dissolves interpersonal subjectivity: 'Love is the I that receives satisfaction

---

114 Hannah Arendt, *The Origins of Totalitarianism* (New York: Harcourt, 1951); Hannah Arendt, *The Human Condition* (Chicago: University of Chicago Press, 1958); Hannah Arendt, *Eichmann in Jerusalem: A Report on the Banality of Evil* (London: Faber and Faber, 1963). Cf. also her *Der Liebesbegriff bei Augustin: Versuch einer philosophischen Interpretation* (Berlin: J. Springer, 1929) and Hannah Arendt, *Het liefdesbegrip bij Augustinus*, translation by Mark Wildschut (Utrecht: Ten Have, 2022). Cf. Peter Venmans, *Amor Mundi: Hoe komen we tot een betekenisvolle relatie met de ander?* (Amsterdam: Atlas Contact, 2016).

115 In Dutch: 'als het ware "opgesloten" in zijn of haar "eigen portret";' Emmanuel Levinas, *Het menselijk gelaat: Essays van Emmanuel Levinas*, gekozen en ingeleid door Ad Peperzak (Utrecht: Amboboeken, 1969), 88–95, 116 and 120; Emmanuel Levinas, *Totalité et infini: Essai sur l'extériorité* (La Haye: Martinus Nijhoff, 1961), 187–190 (*Phaenomenologica* 8).

116 In Dutch: 'Ik denk niet alleen dat hij is, maar ik spreek hem aan'; Levinas, *Het menselijk gelaat*, 91.

from a you, an I that finds in the other the justification of its being. The presence of the other is the whole content of such union.'[117] The face of the other is pithy for Levinas: 'Being – that is man, and only as a neighbour is man accessible. As face.'[118]

This relates to the notion of loving one's neighbour and neighbour law. Levinas' considerations and stance is impressive and appealing. Looking in the face of the other, he states, people cannot overlook the other but must feel the responsibility to relate oneself to the other. The question is how to make this more concrete since people can avoid the challenge or assignment to look the other in the face, or just decline the appeal from the other to recognize him or her, not to speak about doing him or her justice. Or they may look the neighbour straight in the face, but in the meantime, they go their own way without regard to him or her. Nevertheless, deep down, man cannot avoid the face of the other.

4.3 *Speaking about Love*

The face of the other raises questions about our love for the other, how difficult that may be. French philosopher Paul Ricoeur (1913–2005) observed that

117 In Dutch: 'Liefde is het ik dat van een jij voldoening ontvangt, een ik dat in de ander de rechtvaardiging van zijn wezen vindt. De aanwezigheid van de ander is de hele inhoud van een dergelijke verbondenheid'; Levinas, *Het menselijk gelaat*, 116.

118 In Dutch: 'Het zijnde – dat is de mens, en alleen als naaste is de mens toegankelijk. Als gelaat'; Levinas, Het menselijk gelaat, 93 and footnote 57. The French word 'prochain' is translated into Dutch as 'neighbour'. Pepperzak writes: 'Levinas here employs the word prochain, which he prefers not to use until Enigme et phénomène (bibl. 91 and here pp. 192–207), because it indicates too little the Other as other and suggests too much that he is my equal and neighbour. Cf. his own commentary, in this volume p. 196, note 12'; Levinas, *The Human Face*, 235 footnote 57. Levinas avoided the designation 'prochain' because, in his view, it assumed too much 'a community based on proximity (la communauté du voisinage)'. Levinas paid 'attention' only to the suddenness of the disturbance of order by the neighbour as far as he strikes me as 'the first the best'. In Dutch: 'Het Franse woord "prochain" is in het Nederlands vertaald met "naaste". Peperzak schrijft daarover: "Levinas bedient zich hier van het woord *prochain*, dat hij totaan *Enigme et phénomène* (bibl. 91 en hier blz. 192–207) liever niet gebruikt, omdat het teweinig de Ander als ander aangeeft en tezeer suggereert, dat hij mijn gelijke en buur is. Vgl. zijn eigen toelichting, in deze bundel blz. 196, noot 12'; Levinas, *Het menselijk gelaat*, 235 footnote 57. Levinas vermeed de aanduiding 'prochain', omdat het volgens hem te zeer 'een gemeenschap op basis van nabijheid (la communauté du voisinage)' veronderstelde. Levinas lette 'alleen op het plotselinge karakter van de ordeverstoring door de naaste in zover hij mij als "de eerste de beste" overvalt'; Levinas, *Het menselijk gelaat*, 268 footnote 12; Emmanuel Levinas, *Transcendance et Hauteur*: séance du 27 janvier 1962 (Paris: A. Colin, 1962), 73; *Bulletin de la Société français de Philosophie* – (julliet/septembre 1962): 107–108.

it is not easy to talk about love. It may well be too simple and too difficult.[119] One way to transcend extremes is through the dialectic between love and justice. For Ricœur, this meant, first, recognising the initial disproportionality between the two designations and, second, the search for practical mediations that always have the character of fragility and provisionality. For Ricœur, love is 'hypermoral, it enters the practical and ethical sphere only under the aegis of justice'.[120] He ended his contribution on *Love and Justice* with the conclusion and task: 'I would even say that the tenacious incorporation, step by step, of a supplementary degree of compassion and generosity in all our codes – including our penal codes and our codes of social justice – constitutes a perfectly reasonable task, however difficult and interminable it may be.'[121] However difficult the task may be to implement something of compassion and generosity in our codes or laws, it does, however, constitute a 'perfectly reasonable task', according to Ricœur.[122]

It is not enough to incorporate 'something of compassion and generosity in our codes or laws', but it is important to demonstrate also these notions in the application of such codes and laws in daily life whenever we meet the other in the context of 'the dialectic between love and justice'.[123] Paper is patient, it is not sufficient that rules or laws have the nature of a paper tiger. More is needed. It is not impossible to include such notions in law and to apply them, also in a way to be graceful and to express something from grace, even in a secular context, and even if such applications or mediations between love and justice are fragile or provisional.[124] The fragile and provisional nature of these mediations does not absolve people from loving their neighbour, even if this application of the golden rule of loving ones neighbour in a broken world meets its limitation and comes along with the imperfect.

---

119 Paul Ricœur, "Love and Justice," in *Paul Ricoeur: The Hermeneutics of Action*, ed. Richard Kearney (London: Sage, 1996), 23.

120 Ricœur, "Love and Justice," 37.

121 Ricoeur, "Love and Justice," 37.

122 Ricoeur, "Love and Justice," 37.

123 Ricoeur, "Love and Justice," 37.

124 Leon van den Broeke, "A Secular Form of Grace: A Place for Utopia in Law," in *Utopian Thinking in Law, Politics, Architecture and Technology: Hope in a Hopeless World*, eds. Bart van Klink, Marta Soniewicka and Leon van den Broeke (Cheltenham UK: Edward Elgar Publishing, 2022), 76–94.

5 Love, Solidarity, and Law

5.1 *The Reciprocity Principle*

Dutch jurist Dorien Pessers also sought compassion and generosity in law. An expression of this is her advocacy of the right of the other, more specifically, the reciprocity principle. In this section, I endeavour to understand her positioning of this principle in law. In 1999, Pessers received her doctorate from the University of Amsterdam for her dissertation entitled: *Love, solidarity, and law*.[125] In it, she argues for the importance of the reciprocity principle for law. By reciprocity, she thinks of 'a durable relationship of alternating inequality based on intersubjectivity or institutionalised trust in which indeterminate benefits are settled over time.'[126]

The reciprocity principle is about the relationship between legal objects. A legal subject is a bearer of subjective rights and obligations.[127] They may be natural persons but also legal persons (private and public). Under civil law, legal entities may have assets. Legal subjectivity begins at birth and ends at death. I will leave the exception to which Article 1:2 Civil Code refers to here.[128] Besides legal subjects, there are legal objects, who are objects of rights and subjects to the rights of legal objects. A human being cannot be a legal object in the Netherlands. Legal objects are subjects of law. Put differently if there are no legal objects, 'law cannot function'.[129]

---

125 D.W.J.M. Pessers, *Liefde, solidariteit en recht: Een interdisciplinair onderzoek naar het wederkerigheidsbeginsel*, PhD. diss. Universiteit of Amsterdam (Amsterdam: Universiteit van Amsterdam, 1999).

126 In Dutch: 'een duurzame, op intersubjectiviteit of geïnstitutionaliseerd vertrouwen gebaseerde, verhouding van alternerende ongelijkheid waarin onbepaalde prestaties op termijn worden verevend'; Pessers, *Liefde, solidariteit en recht*, 139.

127 H.Ph.J.A.M. Hennekens, "Overheidssubjecten in publiek- en privaatrecht en iets over toerekening van het ene aan het andere subject," in *Vertrouwen in het burgerlijke recht. Liber amicorum prof. mr. S.C.J.J. Kortmann*, eds. S.E. Bartels et al. (Deventer: Wolters Kluwer 2017), par. 16.2.3 (*Onderneming & Recht* 100).

128 'A child of which a woman is pregnant, is regarded to have been born already as often as its interests require so. If it is born lifeless, it is deemed to have never existed'; DCL, "Dutch Civil Code Book 1 Law of Persons and Family Law," accessed 24 September 2024, http://www.dutchcivillaw.com/civilcodebook01.htm.

129 I further leave here the principled legal debate whether law can be without legal subjects; cf. M.J. Kroeze (with the help of H. Beckman and M.A. Verbrugh), ed. *Mr. C. Assers Handleiding tot de beoefening van het Nederlands Burgerlijk Recht. 2. Rechtspersonenrecht. Deel I. De rechtspersoon* (Deventer: Wolters Kluwer 2021) (Asser/Maeijer & Kroeze 2-I* 2015/11); Duco Gerrold Rengers Hora Siccama, *De geestelijke en kerkelijke goederen onder het canonieke, gereformeerde en neutrale recht: Historisch-juridische verhandeling voornamelijk uit Utrechtse gegevens samengesteld,* PhD diss. University Utrecht (Utrecht: s.n., 1905); Hennekens, "Overheidssubjecten in publiek- en privaatrecht," par. 16.2.3.

Pessers draws on French psychoanalyst Jacques Lacan (1901–1981), who argued that there is no direct relationship between two subjects. As Pessers maintains reciprocity involves 'a relationship mediated by a third agency – called the "symbolic order" by Lacan. Through a common symbolic order, the self can reciprocate in the other. Reciprocity is literally understood here as re-reverting'.[130] The notion of reciprocity can be found in the idea of the social contract, which is the basis of the modern legal order, as formulated in the writings of Thomas Hobbes (1588–1679), John Locke (1632–1704) and Jean-Jacques Rousseau (1712–1778).[131] Laws and subjective rights should be established respectively granted as safeguards against aggression (Hobbes), 'invasion of others'[132] (Locke) and 'amour propre' (Rousseau). Aptly, Pessers states, 'The assertiveness of the other is repelled with the shield of law, which obliges to recognise the other. At the same time, the law cancels those differences by bringing both parties as legal subjects under the common denominator of the legal order.'[133] The other is not only the one to whom justice must be done, but the other's assertive desire needs the safeguard of law to secure its own (legal) position. In the reciprocity principle, Pessers distinguishes between mutualism and reciprocity.[134] Mutuality sees reciprocity in the framework of the *do ut des*: I give something so that you give (me) something, derived from Roman religion. Giving had the character of sacrifice. With a human sacrifice, the god(s) would give something in return. People bind themselves to each other only in case they need something from each other. Reciprocity is about the altruistic nature of the relationship based on the principle: *do quia mihi datum est*: I give something because it has been given to me.

According to Pessers, more than 'just' a reciprocity aspect, law also has 'reciprocity potential'. This emerges in private law, labour law and administrative law, especially in contract law, when it comes to principles such as good faith, reasonableness, and fairness. In contract law, parties are first pitted against each other, their interests, legal positions, potential conflicts,

---

130 In Dutch: '[…] een door een derde instantie – door Lacan de "symbolische orde" genoemd – bemiddelde verhouding. Via een gemeenschappelijke symbolische orde kan het eigene in de ander wederkeren. Wederkerigheid wordt hier letterlijk als weder-keren opgevat'; Pessers, *Liefde, solidariteit en recht*, XVI, 2–16.

131 Pessers, *Liefde, solidariteit en recht*, 195.

132 John Locke, *Two Treatises of Government*, pars 123 and 131 (London: Printed for Awnsham and John Churchill, at the Black Swan in Pater-Noster-Row, 1698), 261.

133 In Dutch: 'De geldingsdrang van de ander wordt afgeweerd met het schild van het recht, dat verplicht tot erkenning van de ander. Tegelijkertijd heft het recht die verschillen op door beide partijen *als rechtssubjecten* onder de gemeenschappelijke noemer van de rechtsorde te brengen'; Pessers, *Liefde, solidariteit en recht*, 195.

134 Vgl. Pessers, *Liefde, solidariteit en recht*, 45–52.

and possible faithlessness are identified. Then the parties are joined in a legal relationship.[135]

5.2 *Validity and Recognition Compulsion*

Pessers also highlights the reciprocity principle from the perspective of social reciprocity. She draws on German philosopher and sociologist Alex Honneth, who is concerned with the theory of recognition. In modern law, social reciprocity has undergone a transformation, according to Honneth.[136] He sees this process as a developmental model and links affective reciprocity with *love*, social reciprocity with *life*, and rational reciprocity with *law*. Human beings take risks because the other can be seen as 'a risky attempt at individual self-realisation', according to Honneth.[137] He and Pessers draw on George Wilhelm Friedrich Hegel (1770–1831), among others. Hegel believes that the subject is unable to find a balance in the tension between assertiveness and the compulsion to recognise. This leads to instrumentalisation of the other. Love, however, means 'being oneself in another', or put differently: coming [home] to oneself in the other.[138] This implies turning away doom for the other and adding good to the other.[139]

In line with this, Pessers states, 'In their need for self-respect, people seek the respect and esteem of others.'[140] People want to be respected by others. There is also the assignment to respect the other and his or her rights. This expresses the love for the neighbour.

5.3 *Minimum Peace*

Law has a transformative power in which people are '*irrespective* of personal characteristics and qualities, and *irrespective* of their social group valuation,

135 Pessers, *Liefde, solidariteit en recht*, 195; A.A.G. Peters, "Recht als kritische discussie." In *Recht als kritische discussie: Een selectie uit het werk van A.A.G. Peters*, eds. M.J. Gunning, C. Kelk and C.J.M. Schuyt (Arnhem, Gouda Quint, 1993), 213.

136 A. Honneth, *The Struggle for Recognition: The Moral Grammar of Social Conflicts*, transl. by Joel Anderson (Cambridge: Polity Press, 2005). In German: *Kampf um Anerkennung* (Frankfurt am Main: Suhrkamp, 1992).

137 Honneth, *The Struggle*, 57.

138 Georg Wilhelm Friedrich Hegel, *Phämenologie des Geistes*, 2nd ed., ed. Johann Schulze (Berlin: Verlag von Dunder und Humblot, 1841), 361–362; George W.F. Hegel, "Jena Lectures on the Philosophy of Spirit (1805/1806)," in *Hegel and the Human Spirit: A Translation of the Jena Lectures of the Philosophy of Spirit (1805/1806)*, ed. Leo Rauch (Detroit: Wayne University, 1983), (107)83–183; Pessers, *Liefde, solidariteit en recht*, 12, 197.

139 Cf. Hegel, *Phänomenologie des Geistes*, 361–362.

140 Pessers, *Liefde, solidariteit en recht*, 197.

rationally recognised as subjects of law'.[141] In doing so, law, this 'demanding rational reciprocity [...] forces citizens to recognise the other which they often cannot muster of their own accord, because they cannot recognise themselves in the other'.[142] For Pessers, this broadening of intersubjectivity means: 'Indeed, people need only to recognise each other as subjects of law in order for a minimal peace to be possible. However, this minimal peace is the necessary condition for a broad or reciprocal morality that extends to people outside one's own family or social group.'[143]

5.4 *Legal Certainty and the Principle of Equality*

For Dutch legal philosopher, legal theorist and methodologist Bart van Klink, Pessers' thesis raises the question 'whether the principle of reciprocity [...] is at odds with the principle of legal certainty and whether – as Pessers argues – it offers an alternative to the principle of equality'.[144] The principle of equality assumes that the law treats equal cases equally. According to Van Klink, Pessers 'initially constructs an opposition between reciprocity and equality', but 'gradually she appears to see equality as a precondition for reciprocity'.[145] Law should not be used only instrumentally. When it does, it clashes with the legal principle of reasonableness and fairness. Van Klink ends his review with the probing question 'how can we do justice to another without reverting to our own?'[146] By this, Van Klink is referring to the pitfall of reciprocity that someone starts

---

141 In Dutch: '*ongeacht* persoonlijke kenmerken en kwaliteiten en *ongeacht* de sociale groepswaardering daarvan, op rationele gronden worden erkend als rechtssubject'; Pessers, *Liefde, solidariteit en recht*, 198.

142 In Dutch: 'veeleisende rationele wederkerigheid [...] de burgers tot een erkenning van de ander die zij uit zichzelf vaak niet kunnen opbrengen, omdat zij zich in de ander niet kunnen herkennen'; Pessers, *Liefde, solidariteit en recht*, 198.

143 In Dutch: 'Mensen hoeven elkaar immers slechts als rechtssubjecten te erkennen, teneinde een minimale vrede mogelijk te maken. Deze minimale vrede is echter de noodzakelijke voorwaarde voor een brede of reciproque moraal die zich uitstrekt tot mensen buiten de eigen familiale of sociale groep'; Pessers, *Liefde, solidariteit en recht*, 200.

144 In Dutch: 'of het wederkerigheidsbeginsel [...] niet op gespannen voet staat met het beginsel van rechtszekerheid en of het – zoals Pessers betoogt – een alternatief voor het gelijkheidsbeginsel biedt'; B.M.J. van Klink, "D.W.J.M. Pessers, Liefde, solidariteit en recht: Een interdisciplinair onderzoek naar het wederkerigheidsbeginsel (diss.), Faculteit der Rechtsgeleerdheid UvA, (Amsterdam 1999), 284pp.," *Rechtsfilosofie en Rechtstheorie* 30 (2001): 94–100.

145 In Dutch: 'eerst een oppositie tussen wederkerigheid en gelijkheid', maar 'gaandeweg blijkt ze gelijkheid als een *voorwaarde* voor wederkerigheid te zien'; B.M.J. van Klink, "D.W.J.M. Pessers, Liefde, solidariteit en recht," 99.

146 In Dutch: 'hoe kunnen we recht doen aan een ander zonder het eigene te laten wederkeren?' B.M.J. van Klink, "D.W.J.M. Pessers, Liefde, solidariteit en recht," 100.

filling in what the other person needs. In this way, someone gives back to the other person without doing justice to the other person's own needs. This is a form of appropriation.[147]

This means that loving the other person requires the awareness of not filling in what the other person needs and also not that one gives to the other, because the other gave something to me first. It requires an open attitude to show respect, and to create an open context wherein the other person feels free to express what he-she needs. In this way one can do justice to the love for the neighbour.

6 Law and Theology

The above-mentioned probing question of Bart van Klink can also be illuminated from the perspective of theology of law. The essential task of theology of law is theological reflection on the whole of law, at least when it comes to theology of law in a wider sense. Theology of law in a narrower sense concerns the theology of church law. Theology of law in the broader sense moves in the interdisciplinary discourse of, among others, legal philosophers, socio-legal scholars, legal psychologists, legal economists, and legal methodologists. Theology of law also contribute to that discourse, for instance when it comes to the theological interpretation of the concept-pair of law and grace. Also, this includes what Van Klink as mentioned above raised as the question of self, return and the right of the other, and thus also the relationship between legal subjects, or when the rights of legal subjects are trampled upon. There is no gap between law and grace, between law and faith, between the spiritual and the corporate. Dialectically, they belong together. Grace and justice are not two separate magnitudes. Grace does not cancel out law and justice. Law does not exclude mercy.

This is also what Hans-Richard Reuter seems to conclude. As we have already seen, he does not seem to be positive about and put an end to what he sees as the abstract legal-theological and ecclesiastical drafts of Erik Wolf, Johannes Heckel and Hans Dombois, which he believes are difficult to apply. But does that also conclude that the engagement between love and (church) law is broken? Reuter does not seem to want to give up just yet anyway. For him, from the perspective of Christian faith, the ultimate ground of human justice inside and outside the church can only be the same.[148] The formal structures of church and state can also be the same. The difference lies in what he calls 'the

147 Bart van Klink, exchange of e-mails with Leon van den Broeke, 11 and 12 November 2021.
148 Reuter, "Der Rechtsbegriff," 285.

ultimate grounding of law in the respective conception of the just'.[149] Moreover, Reuter also seems to be mindful not only of Wolf's foundational design, but from the 'Formulierung der Grundsätze des Nächstenrechts' that it is less about principles of a just legal order or a legitimate constitution but about essential virtues for actors in the legal sphere.[150]

Not only Hans-Richard Reuter and Michael Welker, but also Martin Honecker was critical of Wolf's theological foundational design of law in relation to the right of the neighbour:

> In my opinion, the theological approach to law does not open up through the neighbourly relationship of love, but through the insight into the anthropological necessity of law as a protection against injustice and unfairness and as a mediating instance of justice. At the same time, no law, no legal order, no legal principle can mediate love as such.[151]

As critical as Honecker was, however, he believed that Christian love and faith in God, in whose realm people love justice, motivate people to seek genuine justice and justice in law.[152] In doing so, he referred to Psalm 99:4.[153] This is in line with Hegel. Wolfhart Pannenberg refers to him by stating: 'By creating ever new forms of human communion, union of the separated, love brings forth positive law.'[154] Honecker considered the orientation of law towards the subject of law and in bringing and maintaining positive law a task of Christian responsibility for law.

---

149 In German: 'die letzte Begründung des Rechts in der jeweiligen Konzeption des Gerechten'; Reuter, "Der Rechtsbegriff," 285.

150 Reuter, "Der Rechtsbegriff," 257–258.

151 In German: 'Der theologische Zugang zum Recht eröffnet sich meines Erachtens nicht über das Nächstenverhaltnis der Liebe, sondern über die Einsicht in die anthropologische Notwendigkeit des Rechts als Schutz gegen Unrecht und Ungerechtigkeit und als Vermittlungsinstanz von Gerechtigkeit. Zugleich gilt: Kein Recht, keine Rechtsordnung, kein Rechtssatz kann als solcher Liebe vermitteln'; Cf. Honecker, "Recht, Ethos, Glaube," 404.

152 Honecker, "Recht, Ethos, Glaube," 405.

153 Honecker, "Recht, Ethos, Glaube," 404–405; Heinemann, "In Reiches dieses Könings hat man das Recht lieb (Ps. 99,4)."

154 In German: 'Indem die Liebe immer neue Formen menschlicher Gemeinschaft, Verbindung des Getrennten schafft, bringt sie positives Recht hervor'; Wolfhart Pannenberg, "Zur Theologie ins Recht," *Ethik und Ekklesiologie*, ed. Wolfhart Pannenberg (Göttingen: Vandenhoeck und Ruprecht, 1977), 38; Honecker, "Recht, Ethos, Glaube," 405.

7 Church Polity

7.1 *An Assignment*

Martin Honecker's comment noted above and his reference to Psalm 99 also constitute a mission for church law and the church when it comes to (formulating) positive law, and for all those who work for that church and relate to it, if not for all people when it comes to the notion of charity. Faith communities articulate that mission to varying degrees in their regulations. I put this to the test in this section by considering a number of articles from church orders of a wide range of faith communities in succession about normative principles of neighbourliness: the Reformed Churches liberated (*Gereformeerde Kerken vrijgemaakt*), the Protestant Church in the Netherlands (*Protestantse Kerk in the Netherlands*), the Union of Baptist and ABC congregations (*Unie-ABC*) and the Roman Catholic Church.

With this, a brief selection was chosen from the three most common church polity systems (presbyterial-synodal, congregational-independent and episcopal-hierarchical). A brief impression shows that several articles in the church orders of various faith communities are indicative of a church-ordered translation of looking after the other(s). I then relate the notion of symbolic legislation through Bart van Klink's perspective to church orders, ecclesiology and the four-voice model developed by the British practical theologian and expert in congregational studies, social justice and theological action research Helen Cameron and her research colleagues. I elaborate on this notion of the four-voices in faith communities in section 7. With a variation on Van Klink, a church order can be seen as positive, communicative, symbolic legislation that incorporates and respects general principles of good governance. In doing so, a church order ideally considers the polyphony in the faith community, not only of theologians, church policymakers and religious leaders, but also of church members. And a church order is not only normative but is also based on ecclesial practices and aims to be applied in such practices.

7.2 *Reformed Churches Liberated*

The Church Order of the Reformed Churches liberated (*Gereformeerde Kerken vrijgemaakt*) in the Netherlands establishes the equality of both individuals and local churches, Article A2.2.[155] This denomination is the result of a schism in 1944 in the Reformed Churches in the Netherlands (*Gereformeerde Kerken in*

---

155 On 1 May 2023, the Reformed Churches liberated (*Gereformeerde Kerken vrijgemaakt*) re-united with the Netherlands Reformed Churches (*Nederlands Gereformeerde Kerken*) as the schism of 1967. The name of the united church is: Nederlands Reformed Churches

Nederland) and also at the Theological Seminary in Kampen. In 1946, this denomination had 77,303 members and 215 local churches belonged to this denomination.[156] In 2015, there were 120,295 members and 267 local churches. Since the ecclesial schism in 1944, there had been two independent theological schools in Kampen, which later became universities. The church polity motivation below is biblical in nature: 'All are under the one Lord, Jesus Christ, the head of His church.'[157] All this is also in the context that in that church of Christ 'all things should be done in a proper manner and in good order' (1 Corinthians 14:40), 'so that peace may be served', Article 2.1. That peace is not served if one person's right dominates that of another. Office-bearers and church members can easily say 'amen' to the call to peace, but in ecclesial practice easily forget the travail of peace in conflicts. Moreover, biblical peace is not only about being a gift from God through Christ to human beings, but also an assignment to human beings. This assignment cannot be easily overlooked, ignored, or set aside.

> A2 PEACE
> A2.1 In the church of Christ, everything should be done in a proper manner and in good order, so that peace may be served.
> A2.2 All are under the one Lord, Jesus Christ, the head of His church. No person or church may dominate another person or church.[158]

(*Nederlandse Gereformeerde Kerken*). See for the new church order: Nederlandse Gereformeerde Kerken, "Kerkorde en regelingen," accessed 24 September 2024, https://ngk.nl/bestuur-en-organisatie/kerkorde/2.

156 Merijn Wijma, *A Great Multitude One Can Count: A Statistical Study on the Spatio-Temporal Development of the Reformed Denominations in the Netherlands between 1892 and 2015*, PhD dissertation Theological University Kampen, [Amsterdam]: Buijten & Schipperheijn, 2022, 109–123; J. de Graaf and G.J. de Graaf, *50 jaar handboek: Overzicht van predikanten en ledenaantallen in de Gereformeerde Kerken sinds de Vrijmaking*, Goes: Oosterbaan & Le Cointre, 1996, 49.

157 In Dutch: 'Allen staat onder de ene Heer, Jezus Christus, het hoofd van zijn kerk'; GKv, "A. De kerken," accessed 24 September 2024, https://www.gkv.nl/bestuur-en-organisatie/kerkorde/a-de-kerken/.

158 In Dutch: 'A2 VREDE
A2.1 In de kerk van Christus moet alles op gepaste wijze en in goede orde gebeuren, zodat de vrede wordt gediend.
A2.2 Allen staan onder de ene Heer, Jezus Christus, het hoofd van zijn kerk. Geen persoon of kerk mag een andere persoon of kerk overheersen'; GKv, "A. De kerken," accessed 24 September 2024, https://www.gkv.nl/bestuur-en-organisatie/kerkorde/a-de-kerken/. In the new church order of the *Nederlandse Gereformeerde Kerken* this article about maintaining the peace is not included. In a different way the notion of no lordship is formulated in article B1.3; Nederlandse Gereformeerde Kerken, "Kerkorde en regelingen," accessed 24 September 2024, https://ngk.nl/bestuur-en-organisatie/kerkorde/2.

Article F75 also enshrines the right of and for the other, at least in terms of equality of arms for parties. This article of the church of this specific denomination refers to ecclesiastical justice that aims to restore peace through justice. This type of peace is characterised by biblical wisdom and meets the requirements of fair and impartial justice guarantees in particular:

> a. conducting careful investigations;
> b. the application of adversarial proceedings;
> c. the right to be assisted by counsel or adviser;
> d. the possibility of hearing witnesses;
> e. the consultation of experts if necessary
> f. equal access to relevant documents for both parties;
> g. a reasoned written decision;
> h. making provision for urgent situations;
> i. the right to challenge.[159]

This is not merely intended to provide legal cover or to have things properly arranged. Below this lies the notion of looking out for others as members of the congregation and, in doing so, having an eye for the 'salvation and well-being' of others. This applies to people in extraordinary circumstances:

> C49.1 As members of the body of Christ, church members look out for each other in love and serve each other's salvation and welfare in word and deed.

---

159 In Dutch: 'a. het doen van zorgvuldig onderzoek;
b. het toepassen van hoor en wederhoor;
c. het recht om zich te laten bijstaan door een adviseur of raadsman;
d. de mogelijkheid van het horen van getuigen;
e. het zo nodig raadplegen van deskundigen;
f. gelijke toegang tot relevante stukken voor beide partijen;
g. een gemotiveerde schriftelijke uitspraak;
h. het treffen van een voorziening in spoedeisende situaties;
i. het recht van wraking'; GKv "F. Besluitvorming en rechtsmiddelen," accessed 24 September 2024, https://www.gkv.nl/bestuur-en-organisatie/kerkorde/f-besluitvorming-en-rechtsmiddelen/. As such this article is not included in the new church order of the *Nederlandse Gereformeerde Kerken*, although some elements are included in explanation of the national regulations for ecclesiastical jurisdiction, "Kerkorde en regelingen," accessed 24 September 2024, https://ngk.nl/bestuur-en-organisatie/kerkorde/2.

C49.4 The churches make provisions for pastoral care in special situations, such as for people with special disabilities and members who are abroad for some time.[160]

Those who read more precisely cannot fail to notice that it is not just about the 'salvation and well-being' of the other, but about '*each other's* salvation and well-being' (emphasis/italics added, LvdB). With salvation and well-being, the task of deacons in the congregation is implicated. Article B24 seems to focus mainly on the diaconal task of deacons in the congregation, at least if paragraph 2 is considered:

B24 TASK OF DEACONS
B24.1 Deacons shall lead the congregation in the service of mercy and justice in church and world. They encourage mutual care and help as well as Christian commitment and generosity to others in need.
B24.2 The deacons recognise social and material difficulties in the congregation and offer support to the members of the congregation in word and deed. To this end, they visit members of the congregation. They collect charitable gifts, administer them, and distribute them as needed.[161]

Yet, Paragraph 1 of the same article shows that although the diaconal task of deacons is primarily concerned with the congregation, the diaconal scope ex-

160 In Dutch: 'C49.1 De gemeenteleden zien als leden van het lichaam van Christus in liefde naar elkaar om en dienen elkaars heil en welzijn in woord en daad.
C49.4 De kerken treffen voorzieningen voor pastoraat in bijzondere situaties, zoals voor mensen met een bijzondere beperking en leden die voor enige tijd in het buitenland verblijven'; GKv, "C. Het leven van de gemeente," accessed 24 September 2024, https://www.gkv.nl/bestuur-en-organisatie/kerkorde/c-het-leven-van-de-gemeente/. This article is not included as such in the new church order, although some notions are recognizable in article C2 about the life in and of the congregation; Nederlandse Gereformeerde Kerken, "Kerkorde en regelingen," accessed 24 September 2024, https://ngk.nl/bestuur-en-organisatie/kerkorde/2.

161 In Dutch: 'B24 Taak van de diakenen B24.1 De diakenen gaan de gemeente voor in de dienst van barmhartigheid en gerechtigheid in kerk en wereld. Zij stimuleren de onderlinge zorg en hulp alsook de christelijke inzet en vrijgevigheid voor anderen die hulp behoeven.
B24.2 De diakenen onderkennen in de gemeente moeiten in sociaal en materieel opzicht en bieden de gemeenteleden ondersteuning met woord en daad. Zij bezoeken daartoe de gemeenteleden. Zij verzamelen de liefdegaven, beheren die en delen die naar behoefte uit'; GKv, "B. De ambten en overige diensten," accessed 24 September 2024, https://www.gkv.nl/bestuur-en-organisatie/kerkorde/b-de-ambten-en-overige-diensten/. Cf. article B15 of the new church order; Nederlandse Gereformeerde Kerken, "Kerkorde en regelingen," accessed 24 September 2024, https://ngk.nl/bestuur-en-organisatie/kerkorde/2.

tends further. After all, it is about the 'service of mercy and justice in church and world'.[162] Furthermore, I believe it has been accounted for at the Theological University Kampen | Utrecht, reference should be made to the time-honoured Article 31 of the Dordrecht Church Order and also in the version valid from 1978 to 2015 in the Reformed Churches liberated. In the current church order of these churches, the 'old' Article 31 is recognisable in a number of articles scattered in Chapter F. "Decision-making and remedies".[163] This article shows that it wants to take into account the voice of the minority if decisions of church assemblies (church council, classis, particular synod and general synod) (would) go against the Bible or with the church order.[164]

An example of diaconal work of deacons, the other office-bearers (pastors and elders), and church members in church and in society is the Foodbank, a joint project to help those in need and to provide them with food. The same applies to the Clothing Bank when it comes to provide clothes for the needy. Another example is the presence of the church in refugee centres, and the assistance of refugees.[165] At an individual level, deacons and others in church do help individuals both in church and society in a financial and/or material way.

7.3 *Protestant Church in the Netherlands*

The Protestant Church in the Netherlands is the result of the merger in 2004 of the Netherlands Reformed Church (*Nederlandse Hervormde Kerk*), the abovementioned Reformed Churches in the Netherlands (*Gereformeerde Kerken in Nederland*) and the Lutheran Church in the Kingdom of the Netherlands (*Evangelisch-Lutherse Kerk in het Koninkrijk der Nederlanden*).

---

162 GKv, "B. De ambten en overige diensten," accessed 24 September 2024, https://www.gkv.nl/bestuur-en-organisatie/kerkorde/b-de-ambten-en-overige-diensten/.

163 See the transposition table in Deputaten Herziening Kerkorde, "Ontwerp-Werkorde 3: Tekst en toelichting," 2011, 168; GKv, "Kerkorde en historie," accessed 24 September 2024, https://www.gkv.nl/kerkorde-historie/. In de uiteindelijke en geldende tekst van de huidige kerkorde staan ze verspreid onder hoofdstuk 'F. Besluitvorming en rechtsmiddelen'; GKv, "F. Besluitvorming en rechtsmiddelen," accessed 24 September 2024, https://www.gkv.nl/bestuur-en-organisatie/kerkorde/f-besluitvorming-en-rechtsmiddelen/. Cf. chapter 7 of the new church order about 'Decision-making and remedies' of the Nederlandse Gereformeerde Kerken, "Kerkorde en regelingen," accessed 24 September 2024, https://ngk.nl/bestuur-en-organisatie/kerkorde/2.

164 See for an elaboration on the notion of Article 31 Pieter T. Pel, "Artikel 31 DKO in rechtstheologisch perspectief. Hernieuwde kennismaking met een kerkelijke kernbepaling," in *Vast en vluchtig. Kerkrecht in de traditie van Emden 1571*, eds. Klaas-Willem de Jong and Leon van den Broeke, (Kampen: Summum Academic Publications, 2021) (*Deddens Kerkrecht Serie* 5, ed. Leon van den Broeke), 237–272.

165 Cf. Bazuinkerk, "Internationale kerk," accessed 10 March 2024, https://www.bazuinkerk.nl/internationale-kerk/.

In the church order of the Protestant Church in the Netherlands, this right of and for others is expressed, among other things, in Article I.8: 'Sent into the world and called to the ministry of reconciliation, the church bears witness in proclamation and service to all people and nations of salvation in Jesus Christ.'[166] This central notion is elaborated in Article X on the missionary, diaconate, and pastoral care of the church, and Article XVI of the life and the work of the church in ecumenical perspective:

> Article X
> 1. Because of its missionary mandate, the congregation is focused throughout its existence on witnessing and serving those who do not know the Gospel or are alienated from it, so that they too may share in salvation in Jesus Christ.
> 2. The congregation fulfils its diaconal vocation in the church and in the world by sharing what has been given in gifts in the service of mercy and justice, helping where there is no helper and bearing witness to the justice of God where injustice occurs.
> 3. The congregation accomplishes its pastoral task in pastoral care of members and others in need of such care, so that they build each other up in faith, hope, and love.
> 4. In fulfilling its missionary, diaconal and pastoral vocation, the congregation seeks cooperation with other church communities locally.
> 5. With a view to fulfilling its vocation, the congregation shall gratefully make use, in a relationship of reciprocity, of insights and experiences imparted to it by congregations whose members come from other cultures.[167]

---

166 In Dutch: 'Gezonden in de wereld en geroepen tot de bediening van de verzoening, getuigt de kerk in verkondiging en dienst aan alle mensen en aan alle volken van het heil in Jezus Christus'; Protestantse Kerk in Nederland, "Kerkorde," accessed 24 September 2024, https://protestantsekerk.nl/thema/kerkorde/.

167 In Dutch:
'1. De gemeente is vanwege haar missionaire opdracht, in heel haar bestaan gericht op getuigenis en dienst aan hen die het Evangelie niet kennen of daarvan vervreemd zijn, opdat ook zij delen in het heil in Jezus Christus.
2. De gemeente vervult haar diaconale roeping in de kerk en in de wereld door in de dienst van barmhartigheid en gerechtigheid te delen wat haar aan gaven geschonken is, te helpen waar geen helper is en te getuigen van de gerechtigheid van God waar onrecht geschiedt.
3. De gemeente volbrengt haar pastorale taak in de herderlijke zorg aan de leden en anderen die deze zorg behoeven, opdat zij elkaar opbouwen in geloof, hoop en liefde.
4. De gemeente zoekt bij de vervulling van haar missionaire, diaconale en pastorale roeping samenwerking met andere kerkelijke gemeenschappen ter plaatse.
5. Met het oog op de vervulling van haar roeping maakt de gemeente in een relatie van wederkerigheid dankbaar gebruik van inzichten en ervaringen die haar worden aangereikt

> Article XVI
> […] 3. In its diaconal work, in the Netherlands and around the world, the church fulfils its mission to engage with those who suffer and to assist them in seeking solace and justice, in cooperation with churches and congregations locally and with related agencies.[168]

Since there is no more space here to elaborate on equality of arms and the right to a fair trial in the church polity of the Protestant Church in the Netherlands, suffice it to say that just like in the Church Order of the Reformed Churches liberated, the church order of the Protestant Church in the Netherlands also takes into account general legal principles.[169]

7.4 *Union of Baptist and ABC Congregations*

The faith community *Unie-ABC* consist of Baptist and CAMA congregations in the Netherlands. In 2020 this Union-ABC was formed from 'a (for now) administrative merger between the Union of Baptist Churches in the Netherlands ("the Union") and the Alliance of Baptist and CAMA Churches ("ABC")'.[170] The full merger took place in 2023.

Article 3 of the Statutes of the Union of Baptist and ABC congregations states as its purpose:

> a. to promote love, esteem, and cooperation among its members;
> b. to assist the congregations in the performance of their duties and create opportunities to make known the principles of the church and to spread the Gospel;
> c. to cooperate in spreading the Gospel at home and abroad.[171]

---

door gemeenten waarvan de leden uit andere culturen afkomstig zijn'; Protestantse Kerk in Nederland, "Kerkorde," accessed 24 September 2024, https://protestantsekerk.nl/thema/kerkorde/.

168 In Dutch: 'In de diaconale arbeid, in Nederland en in de wereld, vervult de kerk haar opdracht om zich in te zetten voor wie lijden en hen bij te staan in het zoeken naar vertroosting en gerechtigheid, in samenwerking met kerken en gemeenten ter plaatse en met verwante instanties […]'; Protestantse Kerk in Nederland, "Kerkorde," accessed 24 September 2024, https://protestantsekerk.nl/thema/kerkorde/.

169 See for example for general provisions on forms of justice and the right to a fair trial in the Protestant Church in the Netherlands: Klaas-Willem de Jong, "De kerkelijke rechtspraak," in *Nieuwe toelichting op de kerkorde van de Protestantse Kerk in Nederland*, eds. F. Tobias Bos and Leo J. Koffeman (Utrecht: KokBoekencentrum, 2019), 283–311.

170 Translation from Dutch by Leon van den Broeke; Unie-ABC, "Wat is Unie-ABC?," accessed 11 March 2024, https://www.unie-abc.nl/over/wat-is-unie-abc.

171 In Dutch:
'a. onder haar leden liefde, achting en samenwerking te bevorderen;

This article thus includes the promotion of 'love, esteem and cooperation' among its members. Baptist congregations should be focused not only on themselves, but also on their neighbours. This stimulates curiosity about neighbour(s) outside one's own circle of Baptists.

Nonetheless, also the *Unie-ABC* does promote love, esteem, and cooperation outside its own church and aims to make this concrete in specific projects. In 2020 this denomination supported twelve projects of hope, not only in the Netherlands, but also in: church planting in Cuba, supporting students at the theological seminary India, food distribution in Yemen, supporting church leaders in Sierra Leone, playgrounds in Syria, and church planting in Turkey.[172] For Baptists such projects are intertwined with mission work as might already appear from several projects.

7.5 *Roman Catholic Church*

From the canon law book of the Roman Catholic Church, the *Codex Iuris Canonici*, Canon 220 comes to mind with regard to the other outside the church as well: 'No one is permitted to illegitimately harm the good reputation which a person possesses nor to injure the right of any person to protect his or her own privacy.'[173] Canon 223 § 1 seems to focus even more explicitly on people outside their own Church: 'In exercising their rights, the Christian faithful, both as individuals and gathered together in associations, must take into account the common good of the Church, the rights of others, and their own duties toward others.'[174]

This is not only a matter of doctrine, but also of applied ethics in daily practice, to reach out to those in need. This become apparent in the Roman-

b. de gemeenten behulpzaam te zijn in de uitvoering van hun taak en gelegenheden te scheppen om de beginselen van de gemeente bekend te maken en het Evangelie te verbreiden;

c. mede te werken tot verbreiding van het Evangelie in binnen- en buitenland;" Baptisten, "Statuten van de Unie van Baptistengemeenten', accessed 24 September 2024, https://baptisten.nl/images/over-ons/documenten/statuten_unie.pdf.

172 Unie-ABC gemeenten, 'Projecten van hoop: Zendingsprojecten uit de internationale familie 2020', accessed 22 March 2024, https://baptisten.nl/images/nieuws/2020/Zending2020/Projecten_Unie_en_ABC_2020.pdf.

173 The Holy See, "The Code of Canon Law," accessed 24 September 2024, https://www.vatican.va/archive/cod-iuris-canonici/eng/documents/cic_lib2-cann208-329_en.html#TITLE_I.

174 The Holy See, "The Code of Canon Law," accessed 24 September 2024, https://www.vatican.va/archive/cod-iuris-canonici/eng/documents/cic_lib2-cann208-329_en.html#TITLE_I.

Catholic *caritas* in relationship with the catholic social doctrine.[175] *Caritas* is an act of love for one's neighbour, or as pope Benedict XVI put it: 'Love – *caritas* – is an extraordinary force which leads people to opt for courageous and generous engagement in the field of justice and peace.'[176] Caritas, not only for Roman-Catholics, is intertwined with the seven (physical) works of mercy according to the Gospel and the spiritual works of mercy like comforting the grieving and praying for one another.[177]

7.6 *Symbolic Legislation?*

As touched upon at the beginning of this section, the overall impression from several articles in the church orders of various faith communities is that of a church-ordered translation of looking after the other(s). In general, a rule or regulation does not yet have to say much. What matters is not only the positive law, what the rules prescribe, but also what imagination or narrative lies beneath the legislation. Like a law, a church order can also be seen as symbolic legislation. It is not so much about the rule as the story. By way of illustration and analogy, I point to the impressive book by constitutional law scholar Wim Voermans: *Het verhaal van de grondwet* (The Story of the Constitution).[178] He shows that constitutions are not so much about regulation, but about the story they want to tell, also by drawing attention to the legislative historical, social, legal and political context; and yes, even the religious context. This not only applies to the story about the Dutch constitutions. Voermans states:

> So, when it comes to the question of the popularity of the constitution, all sorts of different world experiences suddenly surface alongside "sto-

175 RKKerk.nl, 'Caritas verdieping', accessed 20 March 2024, https://www.rkkerk.nl/caritas/caritas-verdieping/. Cf. also the papal encyclics; RKKerk.nl, 'Caritas verdieping', accessed 20 March 2024, https://www.rkkerk.nl/caritas/caritas-verdieping/#1692175264567-d1e9a469-9ac8. For Caritas international: Youtube, 'Caritas work in 2022', accessed 20 March 2024, https://www.youtube.com/watch?time_continue=7&v=7ZormZynGgk&embeds_referring_euri=https%3A%2F%2Fwww.rkkerk.nl%2F&source_ve_path=MTM5MTE3LDM2ODQyLDIzODUx&feature=emb_title.

176 Vatican, "Encyclical letter caritas in veritate of the supreme pontiff Benedict XVI to the bishops, priests and deacons, men and women, religious, the lay faithful and all people of good will on integral human development in charity and truth," accessed 22 March 2024, https://www.vatican.va/content/benedict-xvi/en/encyclicals/documents/hf_ben-xvi_enc_20090629_caritas-in-veritate.html.

177 Cf. Matthew 25, 31–46; DOCAT, "Wat te doen?," accessed 23 March 2024, https://www.docat.nl/.

178 Wim Voermans, *Het verhaal van de grondwet: Zoeken naar wij*, 4rd ed. (Amsterdam: Prometheus, 2020).

> ries" with explanations. Ideas about living together, working together and organising leadership whose roots go back much further than the Second World War. Ideas and ideologies that have bequeathed centuries and generations to us and that have thus become an increasingly permanent part of our collective consciousness. [...] For the answer to why, we should not look to stories about the constitution [...], but rather to the story of the constitution itself. Where does that story come from, why is it such a strong story, why is it so convincing [...]? In any case, you have little use for a constitution that is little more than a bunch of dead letters on paper. For the ideas, principles, norms, and values of a constitutional system to work [...] its story will have to come alive in the minds and hearts of people who belong to that group. And that means it will have to be told over and over again, endlessly repeated and passed on, using all means at hand: image, sound, imaginary representations. Until it sticks, is held to be true and normal. Until it internalises.[179]

Van Klink seems to concur with this in his work. In his thesis that focuses on symbolic law with open norms for an interpretive and dialogical community, he concludes, 'The law has [...] something symbolic because it is itself a symbol [...] for something "higher".'[180] Such a law contains open norms that act as symbols in the symbolic law that has an idealistic and also an aspirational char-

179 In Dutch: 'Als het gaat om de vraag naar de populariteit van de grondwet komen er naast "verhalen" met verklaringen, dus ook ineens allerlei verschillende soorten wereldbelevingen bovendrijven. Ideeën over samenleven, samenwerken en de organisatie van leiderschap waarvan de wortels veel verder terugreiken dan tot de Tweede Wereldoorlog. Ideeën en ideologieën die eeuwen en generaties aan ons hebben nagelaten en die daarmee een steeds vast onderdeel van ons collectieve bewustzijn zijn geworden. [...] Voor het antwoord op het waarom moeten we niet te rade bij verhalen *over* de grondwet [...], maar juist bij het verhaal *van* de grondwet zelf. Waar komt dat verhaal vandaan, waarom is het zo'n sterk verhaal, waarom is het zo overtuigend? [...] In elk geval heb je weinig aan een grondwet die niet veel meer is dan een boel dode letters op papier. Willen de ideeën, beginselen, normen en waarden van een grondwettelijk bestel hun werk kunnen doen [...] dan zal het verhaal ervan moeten gaan leven in de hoofden en harten van mensen die behoren tot die groep. En dat betekent dat het keer op keer moet worden verteld, eindeloos herhaald en doorgegeven, met alle middelen die ter beschikking staan: beeld, geluid, imaginaire voorstellingen. Totdat het beklijft, voor waar en normaal gehouden wordt. Totdat het internaliseert'; Voermans, *Het verhaal van de grondwet*, 40–41.

180 In Dutch: 'De wet heeft [...] iets symbolisch, omdat ze zelf een symbool [...] is voor iets "hogers"'; Van Klink, *De wet als symbool*, 427. Taal speelt daarin een grote rol; cf. Harold J. Berman, 'Language as an effective symbol of community', in *Law and Language: Effective Symbols of Community*, ed. Harold J. Berman en John Witte Jr., (Cambridge UK/New York: Cambridge University Press, 2013), 36–63.

acter and that are jointly interpreted as symbolic law by 'persons and bodies' involved as an interpretive community.[181] They must then take responsibility. Van Klink distinguishes between negative and positive symbol law.[182] The former involves symbolic legislation in the negative sense, legislation intended in the traditional sense to create a symbol while he considers the positive approach to be 'the communicative approach to legislation'.[183] In that case, a symbol is 'a law that has acquired a special meaning within the legal community of which it is a part'.[184] In short, negative symbol legislation can be characterised as dead letter. It does not function, it is not applied, and it is overlooked. Positive symbol legislation, on the contrary, can be considered as living law. It functions, it is applied, and it is not overlooked. Moreover, it is approved through the times as it moves from worse to better – although ideally.

Symbolic and instrumental legislations need not be mutually exclusive; however instrumental legislation assumes that the ruler assumes that his orders will be followed unconditionally while symbolic legislation assumes a communicative legislature and an interactive and dialogical community.[185] Van Klink sees symbolic legislation as an 'alternative means of steering'. Symbolic legislation in a positive sense can be communicative legislation capable of fulfilling the general principles of proper regulation. Van Klink points out to the Equal Treaty Act as an example of symbolic legislation. Other examples are the Child Law, the Nuisance Law, the Commodities Law, and the Vacancy Law.[186] An example of instrumental law is Traffic law. However, in some cases, and this also applies to Traffic Law, instrumental and symbolic are mixed as can be derived from general clauses such as being a responsible driver.

The same may apply to church orders if they are symbolic legislation in a positive sense capable of fulfilling the general principles of proper regulation. Thereby, church order formulation and the language field of faith communities also listens closely. This is very much the case because church polity requires a cooperation of religious leaders, lawyers, and theologians. There may be a tension between the theological and juridical ways of how to formulate rules in

---

181 In Dutch: 'personen en instanties'; Cf. B.M.J. van Klink, *De wet als symbool: Over wettelijke communicatie en de Wet gelijke behandeling van mannen en vrouwen bij de arbeid*, PhD diss. Tilburg, (s.l.: s.n., 1998) (*Centrum voor wetgevingsvraagstukken*), 427.

182 Cf. Van Klink, *De wet als symbool*, 48ff and 83ff.

183 In Dutch: 'symbol legislation sec' and 'de communicatieve benadering van wetgeving'; Van Klink, *De wet als symbool*, 427.

184 In Dutch: 'een wet die binnen de rechtsgemeenschap waarvan ze deel uitmaakt, een bijzondere betekenis heeft gekregen'; Van Klink, *De wet als symbool*, 427.

185 Cf. Van Klink, *De wet als symbool*, 118ff.

186 Van Klink, *De wet als symbool*, 1.

the church order, and between church leaders or governing bodies and the lay people at the grassroot level. This applies not only to the faith community itself but also to society. This is not always easy because it has to be articulated in a legal format if the narrative under church order 'legislation' is theological, biblical and denominational and is lived out in ministry. Nevertheless, when it is right, faith communities serve not only themselves, including the individual church members, but also those outside the faith community and perhaps even outside the society. If it is good, it is not about a dead letter but a living story. It is not about paper policy but about finding and applying justice to do justice to others as well. It helps if a church order is an expression of communicative law in a positive sense. It may inspire churches to do good in the world, to contribute to the common good, and to avoid the decoy of being church just for the believers, and not for others.

7.7 *Multi-voices Participating in Church*

Moreover, it is not just about regulation nor a nice (or not nice) story of the Church's constitution but also about its application in concrete cases. It is about finding law.[187] Law must always be found and formulated again, applied in concrete situations and to a concrete legal question with the help of legal sources that requires adequate jurisprudence and thus an answer to a legal question. Jurisprudence has developed, in a manner that is increasingly detached 'from the letter of the law, partly as a result of a more complex society, which requires flexible and open legal norms'.[188] This can be considered as problematic and paradoxical. On the one hand office-bearers and church members can require more freedom and less restriction by the church order while on the other hand, they sometimes have a challenging time to deal with the given freedom and to ask for clear rules. It also requires a balance between legal certainty and justice. A legalistic approach may favour legal certainty and result in injustice. Legal autonomy should not lead to arbitrariness. Whereas initially the doctrine of legal finding was concerned 'with the questions of

---

187 Cf. I. Giesen, *Mr. C. Assers Handleiding tot de beoefening van het Nederlands Burgerlijk Recht. Procesrecht. 1. Beginselen van burgerlijk procesrecht* (Deventer: Wolters Kluwer 2015); C.W. Maris en F.C.L.M. Jakobs, *Rechtsvinding en de grondslagen van het recht* (Assen: Van Gorcum, 2011); G.J. Wiarda, *Drie typen van rechtsvinding*, 4rd. ed., ed. T. Koopmans (Deventer: Tjeenk Willink, 1999), 87–91; C.E. Smith, *Regels van rechtsvinding*, 2nd. ed. (Den Haag: Boom Juridische Uitgevers, 2007), 111ff en 189ff.; J.M. Polak, *Theorie en praktijk door rechtsvinding* (Zwolle: Tjeenk Willink, 1953), 48–49.

188 In Dutch: 'van de letter van de wet, onder meer als gevolg van een ingewikkelder samenleving, die soepele en open rechtsnormen vereist'; Maris en Jacobs, *Rechtsvinding en de grondslagen van het recht*, ix and 37.

law interpretation in the more traditional sense of this word', nowadays it is necessary 'to pay attention to the question by which way and by which method the law should be found in the ever-growing area where orientation towards the law is of little or no help to the judge'.[189]

In the context of religious law and faith communities, this means considering more voices than those of a church order or the like. In co-teaching with the scholar of practical theology at the Theological University Utrecht, the Netherlands, Hans Schaeffer, I, like all the students at this university, learned about the four-voice model developed by Helen Cameron and her fellow researchers.[190] It might not come as a surprise that this model includes four voices. The *normative theology* is about the recognition of faith formation and normative presuppositions within one's own tradition. The *formal theology* is that elaborated by theologians. The *operant theology* is the voices of those about the practices themselves. And the *espoused theology* is about faith presuppositions by those who participate in the practice – also ring out when it is right.[191] This model is also helpful to make clear that the topic of this contribution is not just about what church policymakers have made or are making of church polity or church order or what is important to them. It is also about the narrative of what lies beneath it and what views exist in church practice. At least, it can be assumed that there is a theological narrative underneath a church order and that this is translated into church order texts to a greater or lesser extent. As an illustration, I would like to point to the ecclesiological narrative of the Reformed church orders which is about *doctrina et disciplina*. It concerns the Reformed doctrine and the Reformed discipline and admonition. In the sixteenth century, the Reformed theologians had to navigate between the Roman-Catholic Church on the one hand and the Anabaptist church on the other.[192] The Reformers re-

189 In Dutch: 'met de vragen van de wetsinterpretatie in de meer traditionele betekenis van dit woord', thans is het nodig 'aandacht te schenken aan de vraag langs welke weg en langs welke methode het recht moet worden gevonden op het in omvang steeds toenemende gebied waar oriëntatie op de wet de rechter niet of nauwelijks verder helpt'; Maris en Jacobs, *Rechtsvinding en de grondslagen van het recht*, 55.

190 Cf. Helen Cameron, *Talking about God in Practice: Theological Action Research and Practical Theology* (London: SCM Press, 2010).

191 See for example Hans Schaeffer, "Wat is er met de kerkelijke tucht gebeurd? Een onderzoek naar de praktijk van de kerkelijke tucht in de Gereformeerde Kerken (vrijgemaakt)," in *Vast en vluchtig: Kerkrecht in de traditie van Emden 1571*, eds. Klaas-Willem de Jong and Leon van den Broeke (Kampen: Summum Academic Publications, 2021), 118 (*Deddens Kerkrecht Serie* 5, ed. Leon van den Broeke).

192 Cf. Leon van den Broeke, "The Composition of Reformed Church Orders: A Theological, Reformed and Juridical Perspective," in *In die Skriflig/In Luce Verbi* 52/2 (2018), 1–9 https://doi.org/10.4102/ids.v52i2.2351.

jected both church models, the Roman-Catholic canonical law book, but also the spiritual approach of the Anabaptists towards church law.

Furthermore, it is also about how that is lived and applied in the practice of church life and whether legal subjects in the church, church members, guest members and ministers can come along with what church policymakers have or have not decided. The application of this model is helpful here to avoid the decoy of only paying attention to the normative and the formal theology, but also to the operant and the espoused theology, so also to ecclesial practices.

Once again, I return to Erik Wolf and his notion of neighbour law as a fundament for church law. Following Barth, he argued that church law is service law. It should be expressed not only in legislation and church policy but also in its application in practice. Church law is the diaconal order of the neighbourly law.[193] Any service to neighbour is therefore worship.[194]

8 Love Your Neighbour as Yourself!

8.1 *Charity and the Right of the Neighbour*

In this his concluding section, I return to the leading research question – the role of charity in law, theology, and church polity. Erik Wolf is again essential, as one of the three German (church) legal scholars – alongside Johannes Heckel and Hans Dombois – who produced a foundational design for church law. For Wolf, the notion of neighbour's right (*Nächstenrecht*) was fundamental to church law. The law between people flows from divine law, from the relationship between God and man. After several decades in which the aforementioned fundamental designs dominated the German-speaking Church law discourse, this era passed. Hans-Richard Reuter shows that divergent views on the notions of 'church' and 'law' and especially the relationship between those two notions play a role in this. This governs the relationship between church and state.

In the Anglo-Saxon world, around the year 2000, the very relationship between love and law became topical again. American and Western European (legal) philosophers are also concerned with this relationship. For instance, Dorien Pessers draws attention to the relationship between love, solidarity, and law, specifically the reciprocity principle. In Pesser's distinction between the principle of mutuality and the principle of reciprocity, the former seems to fit the task of loving one's neighbour as oneself while the latter takes a step further,

---

193 Wolf, *Ordnung der Kirche*, 511; Steinmüller, *Evangelische Rechtstheologie* 1, 395. Barth, *Die Ordnung der Gemeinde*, 27f.

194 Barth, *Die Ordnung der Gemeinde*, 30.

going an extra mile with respect to the other without demanding, claiming, or expecting anything in return. This raises the question of the *ius constitutum*, the applicable law and invites reflection on living law on the way to the *ius constituendum*, the ideal law. This is equally true of canon law or church polity, which as eschatological law, is law in motion and always in search of even better law. That does not exclude the past, principles, and practices. The command to love our neighbour as ourselves is as old as the church itself. In other words, it has Jewish roots (TaNaKh). The apostolic ideal of the church is the order of love.

A normative, continuous, and insistent appeal from the community of faith to love one's neighbour may fall short of the second half of the double commandment: to love ourselves. Swiss psychiatrist and theologian Michael Pfaff emphasises the importance of this second part. According to him, charity, first, presupposes self-love, that one can take care of oneself: 'Self-love comes before charity. Care for others presupposes well-established care for oneself.'[195] It seems in line with the legal methodology of Bart van Klink who concluded his review of Dorien Pessers' thesis on love, solidarity, and law with the probing question of how we can do justice to another without reverting to self. The trap is that someone thinks he-she knows what the other needs without doing justice to the other's self. That can then be seen as a mode of appropriation. That is not an expression of charity. Intriguing in this context and helpful is Martin Buber's and Franz Rosenzweig's collaborative translation of the double commandment from the Hebrew: 'Love your neighbour, he is like yourself.' This relates to the definition of charity used in section 1 of my contribution, as 'the love of the fellow human being'. This other person, or fellow human being, is like us.

Charity is more general and practical than neighbourly law. The latter designation came into focus because of Wolf's foundational draft of church law. If that is not as tenable as the foundation for the system of church law, the notion of the right of the neighbour is still interesting and relevant and cannot be overlooked. Nevertheless, misunderstandings lurk. Whereas charity is sometimes regarded as fuzzy or fluffy and something of overzealous do-gooders, the perspective of neighbour's right in theology of law and in church polity ideally illuminates something of what is meant by the notion of agape: doing justice to the other. A bill or a church order is patient, but it requires concrete application.

195 In German: 'Selbstliebe kommt vor Nächstenliebe. Fürsorge für andere setzt die gut etablierte Fürsorge für sich selbst voraus'; Michael Pfaff, "Selbstliebe kommt vor Nachstenliebe," *Reformiert* 10 (Oktober 2021): 8.

Besides, charity does not exclude self-love, quite the contrary. Where there is so much focus on self-love, it can be beneficial to see oneself in relation to the other(s) and ideally in a balanced relationship. The notion, the task even, of charity can also be considered realistically by focusing specifically on the (church) legal context, on formulation of law and its application in the social, political, and religious, or philosophical life of every day. Charity law is a (church), legal formulation of charity that provides a legislative framework to recognise the other as a legal subject, as in contract law, but also in church law, and to do justice to the other through compliance and application in everyday practice. Wolf made a plea for this. As far as defining concepts like 'church' and 'law' is concerned, this has been problematic and an obstacle for follow-up research. This does not alter the fact that the notion of neighbour's right is a task. In doing so, Pesser's two elements of the reciprocity principle may be helpful, both the mutualism principle and the reciprocity principle. There may, sometimes must, also need to be attention to one's own legal position in relation to that of the other, in all equality. Church law that seeks to be biblically founded also dares to go a step further, an extra mile, by applying the principle of reciprocity without ignoring its own interests.

This also comes into focus when various church orders of the Reformed Churches liberated, the Protestant Church in the Netherlands, the Union of Baptist Churches and ABC-congregations, and the Roman Catholic Church are questioned from the perspective of neighbour's right. These reveal to a greater or lesser extent the mission of the service of mercy and justice. The focus often seems to be more on one's own church members. Yet here and there, a church order article reaches further and wants to have the other person with his needs and concerns in view and even 'the rights of others, and their own duties toward others' (canon 223 § 1 CIC). This should not just be about one or another Church Order article per se, but also, intrigued by Wim Voermans' story of the constitution,[196] about what the story of a church order is and what the faith community wants to stand for. Or, in the words of Van Klink and translated: a church order as positive, communicative, symbolic legislation that incorporates and respects the general principles of good governance, considering the multi-voicedness in the faith community, not only of theologians, church policymakers and religious leaders but also of church members.

Moreover, the above-mentioned denominations not only emphasize the assignment of loving one's neighbour in both the faith community and in society, but also this remains a divine assignment no matter what the state in a specific country regulates or outsources to charitable institutions, faith communi-

196 Wim Voermans, *Het verhaal van de grondwet*.

ties and individuals when it comes to social welfare. As from the 1950s in the Netherlands, the state took over social welfare from the churches. This raised questions to faith communities what their diaconal task should be. In the past years, however, the state expressed that it needs faith communities and charitable institutions to help the wicked. This raised new questions to faith communities in an era of secularization with a decreasing number of volunteers who can help to make the assignment to love one's neighbour more concrete.

Charity and neighbourly justice can be an expression of salvation in and of institutions; however, the lack of them indicates mischief in and of institutions. A holy faith community is not necessarily a safe faith community. I hope to delve further into neighbour's law not only in research but also in undergraduate, graduate, and postgraduate teaching, not so much as a foundational design but as a notion. Furthermore, I aim to do further research in theology of law, church polity, and the relationship between government and religion through religious law and state law. This includes notions of reasonableness and fairness, good faith (*bona fide*) and bad faith (*mala fide*). In this work, I build on the fruits of study and advice to faith communities, civil society organisations and political organisations, politicians, or individuals therein in recent years.

8.2 *Love Your Neighbour as Yourself!*

The fact that neighbour law as a foundational design of church law can no longer be seen as the beginning, middle and end of church law does not relieve us of the obligation to continue to reflect on the position of the neighbour in legal theological thinking, church law elaboration and codification, and practical application. After all, canon law is diaconal ordering of God's love, or neighbour law. Just for clarification, the neighbour law is not only covered by internal church law but also directed outwardly and externally. The church order does not cover everything in the church. Above all, the notion of order, both of and in the church, is important for the benefit of society and the contribution to the common good.

Let us continue to love our neighbour as ourselves, to be a neighbour to others. This removes the tension in the main title of this publication. The word 'not' should finally be crossed out and the question mark should be replaced by an exclamation mark. Even if Wolf's foundational design for church law is rejected by neighbour law as the centre and foundation of church law, there is still a task of doing justice to the neighbour, not only in paper policy but also in application and observance and even in a complex and hyper-individual society. This applies in both faith communities and society and the academic context. The external pressures of competition and rivalry do not lead to a climate where some consider others more excellent than themselves, to refer to the Apostle

Paul.[197] Competition and rivalry can have a positive effect if it brings out the best in people. It can also lead to ego-driven thinking gaining even more space and/or at the expense of (multi)disciplinary cooperation. A focus on the neighbour can also bring the best out of people.

The double commandment to love our neighbour as ourselves remains in force, in law, theology of law, church polity and beyond. No one is too great to be a little Good Samaritan. Every act of charity and of neighbourly justice is service to God. So indeed, love your neighbour as yourself!

Bibliography

Algra, N.E., and H.R.W. Gokkel. "Pactum." In *Fockema Andreae's verwijzend & verklarend juridisch woordenboek*, eds. N.E. Algra and H.R.W. Gokkel. 12th ed. Groningen: Martinus Nijhoff, 2001.

Althusius, Johannes. *Dicæologicæ libri tres: Totum & universum jus, quo utimur, methodicè complectentes: cum parallelis hujus & Judaici Juris tabulisq[ue] insertis atq[ue] indice triplici, uno, auctorum, altero, capitum singulorum & tertio, rerum & verborum locupletissimo & accuratissimo: opus tam theoricæ quàm praxeos aliarumq́ue facultatum studiosis utilissimum*. Prostant Francofurti: Apud Christophorum Corvinum, [MD]CXVIII.

Arendt, Hannah. *Het liefdesbegrip bij Augustinus*, translation by Mark Wildschut. Utrecht: Ten Have, 2022.

Arendt, Hannah. *Eichmann in Jerusalem: A Report on the Banality of Evil*. London: Faber and Faber, 1963.

Arendt, Hannah. *The Human Condition*. Chicago: University of Chicago Press, 1958.

Arendt, Hannah. *The Origins of Totalitarianism*. New York: Harcourt, 1951.

Arendt, Hannah. *Der Liebesbegriff bei Augustin: Versuch einer philosophischen Interpretation*. Berlin: J. Springer, 1929.

Astorri, Paolo. *Lutheran Theology and Contract Law in Early Modern Germany* (*ca. 1520–1720*). Paderborn: Ferdinand Schöningh, 2019 (*Law and Religion in the Early Modern Period* 1, ed. Herman Selderhuis et al.).

Augustinus, Aurelius. *Schatkamer van het geloof: Preken over teksten uit het Oude Testament* [*Sermones de scripturis 1–50*], eds. Joost van Neer, Martijn Schrama OSA and Anke Tigchelaar. Budel: Damon, 2013.

Baptisten. "Statuten van de Unie van Baptistengemeenten." Accessed 24 September 2024. https://baptisten.nl/images/over-ons/documenten/statuten_unie.pdf.

197 Romans 12:10 and Philippians 2:3.

Barth, Karl. *Die Ordnung der Gemeinde: Zur dogmatischen Grundlegung des Kirchenrechts.* München: Chr. Kaiser Verlag, 1955, 765–824.

Barth, Karl. *Eine Schweizer Stimme, 1938/45.* s.a.: Zollikon 1945.

Bazuinkerk. "Internationale kerk." Accessed 10 March 2024. https://www.bazuinkerk.nl/internationale-kerk/.

Berman, Harold J. "Language as an effective symbol of community." In *Law and Language: Effective Symbols of Community*, eds. Harold J. Berman and John Witte Jr., 36–63. Cambridge UK/New York: Cambridge University Press, 2013.

Berman, Harold J. "The Christian Sources of General Contract Law." In *Christianity and Law: An Introduction*, eds. John Witte Jr. and Frank S. Alexander, 125–142. Cambridge: Cambridge University Press, 2008.

Bible Study Tools. "New International Version (NIV)." Accessed 30 May 2023. https://www.biblestudytools.com/psalms/85.html.

Bonnard, Pierre. *L'Évangile selon Saint Matthieu.* Neuchâtel: Delachaux en Niestlé, 1963 (*Commentaire du Nouveau Testament* 1).

Brinkman, Ronald, and Ilsemarie Breemhaar. "De aanvaarding namens personae miserabiles van een making, waaraan lasten of voorwaarden zijn verbonden." *Weekblad voor Privaatrecht, Notariaat en Registratie* 7263 (2019): 886–893.

Broeder Dieleman. "De liefde is de eerste wet." Accessed 24 September 2024. https://www.youtube.com/watch?v=SiZjC4DYVRo.

Brown, Francis, ed. *The New Brown–Driver–Briggs–Gesenius Hebrew and English Lexicon with an Appendix Containing the Biblical Aramaic.* Peabody Massachusetts: Hendrickson, 1979.

Broyles, Craig C. "Psalms Concerning the Liturgies of Temple Entry." In *The Books of Psalms: Composition and Reception*, eds. Peter W. Flint and Patrik D. Miller, 248–287 Leiden/Boston: Brill, 2005, (*VT Suppl Series* 99).

Buber, Martin, and Frans Rosenzweig. *Die fünf Bücher der Weisung.* Köln/Olten: Hegner, 1954 (*Die Schrift*, verdeutscht von Martin Buber in Gemeinschaft mit Frans Rosenzweig 1).

Buddeus, Johann Franz. *Institutiones theologiae moralis variis obseruationaibus illustratae.* Lipsiae: apud Haeredes Thomae Fritsch, 1727.

Busch, Eberhard. *Die Barmer Thesen 1934–2004.* Göttingen: Vandenhoeck und Ruprecht, 2004.

Calvijn, Johannes. *Institutie of onderwijzing in de christelijke godsdienst* 2. 3rd ed., translated from Latin by A. Sizoo. Delft: W.D. Meinema, [1956].

Calvin, John. *The Institutes of the Christian Religion*, translated by Henry Beveridge. Grand Rapids MI: Christian Classics Ethereal Library, 2002.

Cameron, Helen. *Talking about God in Practice: Theological Action Research and Practical Theology.* London: SCM Press, 2010.

Cattelan, Valentino. *Religion and Contract Law in Islam: From Medieval Trade to Global Finance.* Abingdon, Oxon/New York: Routledge, 2024 (*ICLARS Series on Law and Religion*).

CBN News / Gary Lane. "Hillary Clinton, Progressives and the Freedom to Worship." Accessed 16 May 2024. https://www1.cbn.com/globallane/archive/2016/11/11/hillary-clinton-progressives-and-the-freedom-to-worship.

CCMW. "Research Programme 2018–2023." Accessed 24 September 2024. https://churchandmission.nl/programme/.

CCMW. "Welcome." Accessed 24 September 2024. https://churchandmission.nl/.

Centrum voor Religie en Recht. "Centrum voor Religie en Recht." Accessed 30 May 2023. https://www.religie-recht.nl/.

Chemnitz, Martin. *Loci theologici Dn. Martini Chemnitii, theologi …: qvibvs et Loci commvnes D. Philippi Melanchthonis perspicue explicantur, & quasi integrum Christianæ doctrinæ corpus, ecclesiæ Dei sinceré proponitur*, ed. Polycarpus Leyser. Francofvrti: Typis & sumptibus Ioannis Spiessij, 1604.

Cochran, Robert F. Jr., and Zachary R. Calo, eds. *Agape, Justice and Law: How Might Christian Love Shape Law?* Cambridge: Cambridge University Press, 2017 (*Cambridge Studies in Law and Christianity*, ed. John Witte Jr.).

"Codex Iuris Canonci." Accessed 24 September 2024. https://www.rkdocumenten.nl/rkdocs/.

Coenen, Lothar, Erich Beyreuther and Hans Bietenhard, eds. *Theologisches Begriffslexikon zum Neuen Testament*, 2nd ed. Wuppertal: Theologischer Verlag Rolf Brockhaus, 1970.

College voor de Rechten van de Mens. "Home." Accessed 7 June 2024. https://www.mensenrechten.nl/.

Day, John. *Psalms.* London: T&T Clark, 1999.

DCL. "Dutch Civil Code Book 1 Law of Persons and Family Law." Accessed 30 May 2023. http://www.dutchcivillaw.com/civilcodebook01.htm.

Deddens, P. "Veel kerk en weinig recht? II." *De Reformatie* 26, no. 2 (14 October 1950): 28–30.

Deddens, P. "Veel kerk en weinig recht? I." *De Reformatie* 26, no. 1 (7 October 1950): 17.

De Graaf, J. and G.J. de Graaf. *50 jaar handboek: Overzicht van predikanten en ledenaantallen in de Gereformeerde Kerken sinds de Vrijmaking.* Goes: Oosterbaan & Le Cointre, 1996.

De Jong, Klaas-Willem. "De kerkelijke rechtspraak." In *Nieuwe toelichting op de Kerkorde van de Protestantse Kerk in Nederland*, eds. F. Tobias Bos and Leo J. Koffeman, 283–311. Utrecht: KokBoekencentrum, 2019.

Den Boon, Ton, Dirk Geeraerts and Nicoline van der Sijs, eds. *Van Dale Groot woordenboek van de Nederlandse taal* 2. 14th ed. Utrecht/Antwerpen: Van Dale Lexicografie, 2005.

DOCAT. "Wat te doen?" Accessed 23 March 2024. https://www.docat.nl/.

Dombois, Hans. *Das Recht der Gnade.* 3 Vols. Bielefeld: Luther-Verlag, 1961–1983.

Dreier, Ralf. "Entwicklungen und Probleme der Rechtstheologie." *Zeitschrift für Evangelisches Kirchenrecht* 25 (1980): 20–39.

Duve, Thomas. *Studien zum ius singulare und den privilegia miserabilium personarum, senum und indorum in Alter und Neuer Welt.* Frankfurt am Main: Klostermann 2008 (*Studien zur europäischen Rechtsgeschichte* 231).

Eisermann, Johannes. *Jo. Ferrarii, Montani, adnotationes in IIII Institutionum Iustiniani libros.* Apud Marpurgum: [Fran. Rhodus excudebat], xiij kal. April. añ. xxxij [20 Mar. 1532].

Fockema Andreae, Sybrandus J. *Oud-Nederlandsch Burgelijk Recht.* Vol. 2. Haarlem: Bohn, [1906].

Gibbs, Jeffrey A. *Matthew 11:2–20:34.* Saint Louis: Concordia Publishing House, 2010 (*Concordia Commentary*).

Giesen, I. *Mr. C. Assers Handleiding tot de beoefening van het Nederlands Burgerlijk Recht: Procesrecht. 1. Beginselen van burgerlijk procesrecht.* Deventer: Wolters Kluwer, 2015.

Gilabert, Pablo. *Human Dignity and Human Rights.* Oxford: Oxford University Press, 2018.

Gispen, W.H. *Leviticus.* Kampen: Kok, 1950 (*Commentaar op het Oude Testament*).

GKv. "A. De kerken." Accessed 24 September 2024. https://www.gkv.nl/bestuur-en-organisatie/kerkorde/a-de-kerken/.

GKv. "B. De ambten en overige diensten." Accessed 24 September 2024. https://www.gkv.nl/bestuur-en-organisatie/kerkorde/b-de-ambten-en-overige-diensten/.

GKv. "C. Het leven van de gemeente." Accessed 24 September 2024. https://www.gkv.nl/bestuur-en-organisatie/kerkorde/c-het-leven-van-de-gemeente/.

GKv. "F. Besluitvorming en rechtsmiddelen." Accessed 24 September 2024. https://www.gkv.nl/bestuur-en-organisatie/kerkorde/f-besluitvorming-en-rechtsmiddelen/.

Gkv. "Kerkorde en historie." Accessed 24 September 2024. https://www.gkv.nl/kerkorde-historie/.

A Greek-English Lexicon of the New Testament and Other Early Christian Literature: A Translation and Adaption of the Fourth Revised and Augmented Edition of Walter Bauer's Griechisch-Deutsches Wörterbuch zu den Schriften des Neuen Testaments und der übrigen urchristlichen Literatur, eds. William F. Arndt and F. Wilburg Gingrich. 2nd ed., eds. F. Wilburg Gingrich and Frederick W. Danker. Chicago/London: The University of Chicago Press, 1979.

Harinck, George. *Tussen Barmen en Amsterdam: Rede uitgesproken op vrijdag 6 juni 2003 in de Burgwalkerk te Kampen bij de aanvaarding van het ambt van bijzonder hoogleraar namens het Archief- en Documentatiecentrum in de geschiedenis van de Gereformeerde Kerken in de context van het Nederlands protestantisme aan de The-*

ologische Universiteit van de Gereformeerde Kerken in Nederland. Amstelveen: EON Pers, 2003.

Heckel, Johannes. *Lex charitatis: Eine juristische Untersuchung über das Recht in der Theologie Martin Luthers*, ed. Martin Heckel. 2nd ed. Köln/Wien: Böhlau Verlag, 1973.

Heckel, Johannes. *Das blinde, undeutliche Wort 'Kirche': Gesammelte Aufsätze*, ed. Siegfried Grundmann, Köln/Graz: Böhlau Verlag, 1964.

Hegel, George W.F. "Jena Lectures on the Philosophy of Spirit (1805/1806)." In *Hegel and the Human Spirit: A Translation of the Jena Lectures of the Philosophy of Spirit (1805/1806)*, ed. Leo Rauch, 83–183. Detroit: Wayne University, 1983.

Hegel, Georg Wilhelm Friedrich. *Phämenologie des Geistes*, 2nd ed., ed. Johann Schulze. Berlin: Verlag von Dunder and Humblot, 1841.

Heinemann, Gustav. "Im Reiches dieses Könings hat man das Recht lieb (Ps. 99,4)." In Gustav W. Heinemann, *Glaubensfreiheit – Bürgerfreiheit. Reden und Aufsätze Kirche – Staat – Gesellschaft 1945–1975*, ed. Diether Koch, 124–132. 2nd ed. München: Chr. Kaiser, 1990/*Die Stimme der Gemeinde* 6 (1954).

Hemmingsen, Niels. *De lege naturae apodictica methodus concinnata per Nicolaum Hemmingium.* Witebergae: excudebant Haeredes Georgij Rhau, 1562.

Hennekens, H.Ph.J.A.M. "Overheidssubjecten in publiek- en privaatrecht en iets over toerekening van het ene aan het andere subject." In *Vertrouwen in het burgerlijke recht: Liber amicorum prof. mr. S.C.J.J. Kortmann*, eds. S.E. Bartels et al. Deventer: Wolters Kluwer 2017, par. 16.2.3 (*Onderneming & Recht* 100).

Hiebsch, Sabine. "Luther en (kerk)recht: Een verkenning." In *Geest of Recht? Kerkrecht tussen ideaal en werkelijkheid*, eds. Leon van den Broeke and Hans Schaeffer, 13–34. Kampen: Summum Academic Publications, 2019 (*Deddens Kerkrecht Serie* 3, ed. Leon van den Broeke).

The Holy See. "The Code of Canon Law." Accessed 30 May 2023. https://www.vatican.va/archive/cod-iuris-canonici/eng/documents/cic_lib2-cann208-329_en.html#TITLE_I.

Hollerbach, Alexander. "In memoriam Erik Wolf †." *Zeitschrift der Savigny-Stiftung für Rechtsgeschichte/Kanonistische Abteilung* 65 (1979): 460.

Honecker, Martin. "Recht, Ethos, Glaube." *Zeitschrift für evangelisches Kirchenrecht* 29 (1984): 383–405.

Honneth, A. *The Struggle for Recognition: The Moral Grammar of Social Conflicts*, translated by Joel Anderson. Cambridge: Polity Press, 2005. Original *Kampf um Anerkennung*, Frankfurt am Main, 1992.

Jagersma, Henk. *"Leviticus 19": Identiteit, bevrijding, gemeenschap.* PhD dissertation University Utrecht. Assen: Van Gorcum & Comp./H.J. Prakke and H.M.G. Prakke, [1972].

Instituut voor de Nederlandse Taal. "Historische woordenboeken." Accessed 24 September 2024, https://gtb.ivdnt.org.

Jendri, Alwast. *Dialektik und Rechtstheologie: Eine Grundlagenuntersuchung zu Ansatz und Methode der rechtstheologischen Konstruktion "Christokratie und Bruderschaft" von Erik Wolf*. Köln/Wien: Böhlau, 1985.

Karan, P.P. *The Non-western World: Environment, Development, and Human Rights*. New York: Taylor & Francis, 2005.

Kiuchi, Nobuyoshi. *Leviticus*. Nottingham/Downers Grove, Illinois: Apollos/Inter-Varsity Press, 2007 (*Apollos Old Testament Commentary*, eds. David W. Baker and Gordon J. Wenham 3).

Kleinig, John W. *Leviticus*. Saint Louis: Concordia Publishing House, 2003 (*Concordia Commentary: A Theological Exposition of Sacred Scripture*).

Koffeman, Leo J. *In Order to Serve: An Ecumenical Introduction to Church Polity*, Zürich: LIT Verlag, 2014 (*Church Polity and Ecumenism: Global Perspectives* 1, eds. Leo J. Koffeman, Allan J. Janssen and Johannes Smit).

Kretzmer, David and Ekhart Klein, eds. *The Concept of Human Dignity in Human Rights Discourse*. The Hague: Kluwer Law International, 2002.

Kroeze, M.J. (with H. Beckman and M.A. Verbrugh). *Mr. C. Assers Handleiding tot de beoefening van het Nederlands Burgerlijk Recht: 2. Rechtspersonenrecht. Deel I. De rechtspersoon*. Deventer: Wolters Kluwer, 2021 (Asser/Maeijer & Kroeze 2-I* 2015/11).

Kuyk, J. "Marck, Frederik Adolf, van der." In *Nieuw Nederlandsch Biografisch Woordenboek* 3, eds P.C. Molhuysen and P.J. Blok, 816–819. Leiden: A.W. Sijthoff, 1914.

Lessing, Eckhard. "Das Verständnis der Ökumene im deutschen evangelischen Kirchenrecht nach dem 2. Weltkrieg." In *Kirche-Recht-Ökumene: Studien zur Ekklesiologie*, ed. Eckhard Lessing, 134–152. Bielefeld: Luther-Verlag, 1982.

Levinas, Emmanuel. *Het menselijk gelaat: Essays van Emmanuel Levinas*, ed. Ad Peperzak. Utrecht: Amboboeken, 1969.

Levinas, Emmanuel. *Transcendance et Hauteur*: Séance du 27 janvier 1962, 73. Paris: A. Colin, 1962/ *Bulletin de la Société français de Philosophie* (July/September 1962).

Levinas, Emmanuel. *Totalité et infini: Essai sur l'extériorité*. La Haye: Martinus Nijhoff, 1961 (*Phaenomenologica* 8).

Locke, John. *Two Treatises of Government*, pars 123 and 131. London: Printed for Awnsham and John Churchill, at the Black Swan in Pater-Noster-Row, 1698.

Luther, Martin. *Von der Freiheit eines Christenmenschen = De libertate Christiana*, ed. Reinhold Rieger. Tübingen: Mohr Siebeck, 2007 (*Kommentare zu Schriften Luthers* 1).

Luther, Martin. "An die Pfarrherrn, wider den Wucher zu predigen." (1540). In WA 51, 331–424.

Luther, Martin. "Die Thesen." (1539). In WA 39II, 39–91.

Luther, Martin. "Tischreden Doct. Mart. Luthers von Juristen." (1531–1546). In WA 6Ti, no. 7013, 326.

Luther, Martin. "Fastenpostille 1525, Epistel auf den 4. Sonntage nach Epiphanias Rom. 13ff." In WA 17II, 102, 8–12.

Luther, Martin. “Von Kaufshandlung und Wucher.” (1524). In WA 15, 293–313.

Luther, Martin. “Von Weltlicher Oberheit, wie weit man ihr Gehorsam schuldig sei.” (1523). In WA 11, 280, 13–19 and 245–81.

Luther, Martin. “Das Magnificat verdeutschet und ausgelegt.” (1521). In WA 7, 583, 15–16.

Luther, Martin. “Das Magnificat verdeutschet und ausgelegt.” (1521). In WA 7, 582, 19ff.

Luther, Martin. “Ein (Grosser) Sermon von dem Wucher.” (1520). In WA 6, 36–60.

Luther, Martin. “An den Christlichen Adel deutscher Nation von des Christlichen Standes besserung.” (1520). In WA 6, 459, 26–29.

Luther, Martin. “(Kleiner) Sermon van dem Wucher.” (1519). In WA 6, 3–8.

Luther, Martin. “Vorlesungen über 1. Mose von 1535–45.” (1535–1545). In WA 42, 356, 22.

Mäkinen, Virpi et al. eds. *Rights at the Margins: Historical, Legal and Philosophical Perspectives*. Leiden/Boston: Brill, 2020 (*Brill's Studies in Intellectual History* 316).

Maris, C.W., and F.C.L.M. Jakobs, *Rechtsvinding en de grondslagen van het recht*, 2nd ed. Assen: Van Gorcum, 2011.

Mayer, A. “Redefining rights: OIC attempts to reshape values in the UN human rights system.” In *Routledge Handbook on Human Rights and the Middle East and North Africa*, ed. T. Chase, 170–181. London: Routledge: 2017.

Melanchton, Philip. *Opera Quae Supersunt Omnia*, ed. Heinrich Ernst Bindseil. Brunsvigae: apud C.A. Schwetschke et filium, 1855 (*Corpus Reformatorum* XXII).

Melanchton, Philip. *Opera Quae Supersunt Omnia*, ed. Heinrich Ernst Bindseil. Brunsvigae: apud C.A. Schwetschke et filium, 1854 (*Corpus Reformatorum* XXI).

Mende, Janne. “Are human rights western – And why does it matter? A perspective from international political theory.” *Journal of International Political Theory* 17, no. 1 (2019). Accessed 14 June 2024. https://doi.org/10.1177/1755088219832992.

Müller, Christine-Ruth. *Bekenntnis und Bekennen: Dietrich Bonhoeffer in Bethel (1933). Ein lutherischer Versuch*. München: Kaiser, 1989.

Nederlandse Gereformeerde Kerken. “Kerkorde en regelingen.” Accessed 7 June 2023. https://ngk.nl/bestuur-en-organisatie/kerkorde/2.

Novum Testamentum Graece (*NA28*). Stuttgart: Deutsche Bibelgesellschaft, 2012. Accessed 24 September 2024. https://www.academic-bible.com/en/online-bibles/novum-testamentum-graece-na-28/read-the-bible-text/bibel/text/lesen/stelle/50/190001/199999/ch/7946f9f7f5fcda8de294600d3307c3b8/.

Oldendorp, Johannes. *Wat byllich ist und recht: Die deutsche Erstlingsschrift des sogenannten Naturrechts*. Frankfurt/Main, Sauer & Auvermann, 1969, reprint of the ed. published in Rostock in 1529, introduction A. Freybe.

Oord, Thomas Jay. *The Nature of Love: A Theology*. St. Louis MO: Chalice Press, 2010.

Pannenberg, Wolfhart. “Zur Theologie ins Recht.” In *Ethik und Ekklesiologie: Gesammelte Aufsätze*, edited by Wolfhart Pannenberg, 11–40. Göttingen: Vandenhoeck und Ruprecht, 1977.

Pel, Pieter T. "Artikel 31 DKO in rechtstheologisch perspectief: Hernieuwde kennismaking met een kerkelijke kernbepaling." In *Vast en vluchtig: Kerkrecht in de traditie van Emden 1571*, eds. Klaas-Willem de Jong and Leon van den Broeke, 237–272. Kampen: Summum Academic Publications, 2021 (*Deddens Kerkrecht Serie* 5, ed. Leon van den Broeke).

Pepperdine | Casuro School of Law. "Love and law." Accessed 24 September 2024. https://law.pepperdine.edu/nootbaar-institute/annual-conference/loveandlaw.

Pessers, D.W.J.M. *Liefde, solidariteit en recht: Een interdisciplinair onderzoek naar het wederkerigheidsbeginsel.* PhD diss. University of Amsterdam. Amsterdam: Universiteit van Amsterdam, 1999.

Peters, A.A.G. "Recht als kritische discussie." In *Recht als kritische discussie: Een selectie uit het werk van A.A.G. Peters*, eds. M.J. Gunning, C. Kelk and C.J.M. Schuyt, 209–238. Arnhem: Gouda Quint, 1993.

Pfaff, Michael. "Selbstliebe kommt vor Nächstenliebe," *Reformiert* 10 (oktober 2021): 8.

Plöchl, Willibald M. *Geschichte des Kirchenrechts.* 2nd ed. Wien/München: Herold, 1960.

Polak, J.M. *Theorie en praktijk door rechtsvinding*. Zwolle: Tjeenk Willink, 1953.

Přibáň, Jiří. *Constitutional Imaginaries: A Theory of European Societal Constitutionalism.* London/New York: Routledge, Taylor and Francis Group, 2021.

Protestantse Kerk in Nederland. "Kerkorde." Accessed 24 September 2024. https://protestantsekerk.nl/thema/kerkorde/.

Rau, Gerhard, Hans-Richard Reuter and Klaus Schlaich, eds. *Das Recht der Kirche.* 3 Vols. Gütersloh: Chr. Kaiser/Gütersloher Verlagshaus, 1994–1997 (*Forschungen und Berichte der Evangelischen Sudiengemeinschaft* 49–51, im Auftrag des Wissenschaftlichen Kuratoriums, ed. Heinz Wismann).

Rengers Hora Siccama, Duco Gerrold. *De geestelijke en kerkelijke goederen onder het canonieke, gereformeerde en neutrale recht: Historisch-juridische verhandeling vooramelijk uit Utrechtse gegevens samengesteld.* PhD diss. Utrecht. Utrecht: s.n., 1905.

Reuter, Hans-Richard. "Der Rechtsbegriff des Kirchenrechts in systematisch-theologischer Sicht." In *Das Recht der Kirche: Band 1 Zur Theorie des Kirchenrechts*, eds. Gerhard Rau, Hans-Richard Reuter and Klaus Schlaich, 236–286. Gütersloh: Chr. Kaiser Gütersloher Verlagshaus (*Forschungen und Berichte der Evangelischen Studiengemeinschaft. Im Auftrag des Wissenschaftlichen Kuratoriums* 49, ed. Heinz Wismann).

Ricœur, Paul. "Love and Justice." In *Paul Ricoeur: The Hermeneutics of Action*, ed. Richard Kearney, 23–39. London: Sage, 1996.

Ridderbos, Herman. *De komst van het koninkrijk: Jezus' prediking volgens de synoptische evangeliën.* 3rd ed. Kampen: Kok, 1985.

RKKerk.nl. "Caritas verdieping." Accessed 20 March 2024. https://www.rkkerk.nl/caritas/caritas-verdieping/.

Robbers, Gerhard. "Grundsatzfragen der heutigen Rechtstheologie." *Zeitschrift für evangelisches Kirchenrecht* 37 (1992/3): 230–240.

Schaeffer, Hans. "Wat is er met de kerkelijke tucht gebeurd? Een onderzoek naar de praktijk van de kerkelijke tucht in de Gereformeerde Kerken (vrijgemaakt)." In *Vast en vluchtig: Kerkrecht in de traditie van Emden 1571*, eds. Klaas-Willem de Jong and Leon van den Broeke, 115–148. Kampen: Summum Academic Publications, 2021 (*Deddens Kerkrecht Serie* 5, ed. Leon van den Broeke).

Schilder, Klaas. "Kerkverband en kerkverbond." In K. Schilder. *Verzamelde werken 1944–1945*, eds. G. Harinck and W.G. de Vries, 17–35. Barneveld: De Vuurbaak, 2001.

Schilder, Klaas. "Persschouw." *De Reformatie* 19, no. 6 (11 november 1938): 47–48.

Smith, C.E. *Regels van rechtsvinding*. 2nd ed. Den Haag: Boom Juridische Uitgevers, 2007.

Sohm, Rudolph. *Kirchenrecht I: Die historische Grundlagen*. Leipzig: Verlag von Duncker & Humblot, 1892.

Steinmüller, Wilhelm. *Evangelische Rechtstheologie: Zweireichelehre. Christokratie. Gnadenrecht* 1. Köln/Graz: Böhlau Verlag, 1968.

Turner, David L. *Matthew*. Grand Rapids MI: Baker Academic: 2008 (*Baker Exegetical Commentary on the New Testament*).

Unie-ABC gemeenten. "Projecten van hoop: Zendingsprojecten uit de internationale familie 2020." Accessed 22 March 2024. https://baptisten.nl/images/nieuws/2020/Zending2020/Projecten_Unie_en_ABC_2020.pdf.

Unie-ABC. "Wat is Unie-ABC?" Accessed 11 March 2024. https://www.unie-abc.nl/over/wat-is-unie-abc.

United Nations Human Rights Office of the High Commissioner. "International Covenant on Civil and Political Rights." Accessed 16 May 2024. https://www.ohchr.org/en/instruments-mechanisms/instruments/international-covenant-civil-and-political-rights.

United Nations, "Universal Declaration on Human Rights." Accessed 30 May 2023. https://www.un.org/en/about-us/universal-declaration-of-human-rights.

Universität Freiburg. "Über das Institut." Accessed 29 January 2024. https://www.jura.uni-freiburg.de/de/institute/rphil/institut/ueber_das_institut?set_language=de.

Universiteitsbibliotheek Gent, "Decretum Gratiani." Accessed 24 September 2024. https://lib.ugent.be/en/catalog/rug01:000794409.

Van den Broeke, Leon. "A Secular Form of Grace: A Place for Utopia in Law." In *Utopian Thinking in Law, Politics, Architecture and Technology: Hope in a Hopeless World*, eds. Bart van Klink, Marta Soniewicka and Leon van den Broeke, 76–94. Cheltenham UK: Edward Elgar Publishing, 2022.

Van den Broeke, Leon. "'Fear God, Honour the Emperor': The Barmen Declaration and its Reception in the Netherlands." In *Naaste verwanten/Nahe Verwandte: Het gereformeerde protestantisme in Nederland en Duitsland in de twintigste eeuw/Der reformierte Protestantismus in den Niederlanden und in Deutschland im 20. Jahrhundert*, eds. George Harinck and Hans-Georg Ulrichs, 161–189. Amersfoort: De Vuurbaak, 2020, (*ADChartasreeks* 36, ed. George Harinck).

Van den Broeke, Leon. "Het recht volgt het leven? Van wetboek en kerkorde naar kunstwerk en liedboek." In *Geest of Recht? Kerkrecht tussen ideaal en werkelijkheid*, eds. Leon van den Broeke and Hans Schaeffer, 95–112. Kampen: Summum Academic Publications, 2019 (*Deddens Kerkrecht Serie* 3, ed. Leon van den Broeke).

Van den Broeke, Leon "The Composition of Reformed Church Orders: A Theological, Reformed and Juridical Perspective." *In die Skriflig/In Luce Verbi* 52/2 (2018), 1–9 https://doi.org/10.4102/ids.v52i2.2351.

Van der Marck, Frederik A. *Lectiones Academicae*. Groningae: Hajo Spandaw, 1771–1776.

Van Klink, Bart. Exchange of e-mails with Leon van den Broeke. 11 and 12 November 2021.

Van Klink, B.M.J. [Bart]. "D.W.J.M. Pessers, Liefde, solidariteit en recht Een interdisciplinair onderzoek naar het wederkerigheidsbeginsel (diss.), Faculteit der Rechtsgeleerdheid UvA, Amsterdam 1999, 284pp." *Rechtsfilosofie en Rechtstheorie* 30 (2001): 94–100.

Van Klink, B.M.J. [Bart]. *De wet als symbool: Over wettelijke communicatie en de Wet gelijke behandeling van mannen en vrouwen bij de arbeid*, PhD. diss. Tilburg. s.l.: s.n., 1998 (*Centrum voor wetgevingsvraagstukken*).

Vatican. "Encyclical letter caritas in veritate of the supreme pontiff Benedict XVI to the bishops, priests and deacons, men and women, religious, the lay faithful and all people of good will on integral human development in charity and truth." Accessed 22 March 2024. https://www.vatican.va/content/benedict-xvi/en/encyclicals/documents/hf_ben-xvi_enc_20090629_caritas-in-veritate.html.

Veenhof, Jan. *Geist und Liebe: Die systematischen Voraussetzungen der Ethik Hendrik van Oyens*. Amsterdam: Rodopi, 1978.

Venmans, Peter. *Amor Mundi: Hoe komen we tot een betekenisvolle relatie met de ander?* Amsterdam: Atlas Contact, 2016.

Vermeersch, Griet. "'Miserabele personen' en hun toegang tot het stadsbestuur." *Low Countries Journal of Social and Economic History* 12, no. 4 (2015): 1–27.

Voermans, Wim. *Het verhaal van de grondwet: Zoeken naar wij*. 4th ed. Amsterdam: Prometheus, 2020.

WA: Luther, Martin. *Werk: Kritische Gesamtausgabe*. Weimar: Hermann Böhlaus, 1883ff.

Welker, Michael. "Recht in den biblischen Überlieferungen in systematisch-theologischer Sicht." In *Das Recht der Kirche: Band I Zur Theorie des Kirchenrechts*, eds. Gerhard Rau, Hans-Richard Reuter and Klaus Schlaich, 390–414 (Gütersloh: Chr. Kaiser/Gütersloher Verlagshaus, 1994–1997) (*Forschungen und Berichte der Evangelischen Sudiengemeinschaft* 49, im Auftrag des Wissenschaftlichen Kuratoriums, ed. Heinz Wismann).

Wiarda, G.J. *Drie typen van rechtsvinding*. 4th ed., ed. T. Koopmans, 87–91. Deventer: Tjeenk Willink, 1999.

Wijma, Merijn. *A Great Multitude One Can Count: A Statistical Study on the Spatio-Temporal Development of the Reformed Denominations in the Netherlands between 1892 and 2015*. PhD dissertation Theological University Kampen. [Amsterdam]: Buijten & Schipperheijn, 2022.

Winroth, Anders. *The making of Gratian's Decretum*. Cambridge: Cambridge University Press, 2000.

Witte Jr., John and Michael Green. "Religious Freedom, Democracy, and International Human Rights." In *Rethinking Religion and World Affairs*, eds. by Timothy Samuel Shah, Alfred Stephan, and Monica Duffy Toft, 104–124. Oxford: Oxford University Press, 2012.

Witte Jr., John. *The Reformation of Rights Law: Religion and Human Rights in Early Modern Calvinism*. Cambridge / New York: Cambridge University Press, 2007.

Wolf, Erik, *Rechtsphilosophische Studien*, ed. Alexander Hollerbach. Frankfurt am Main: Klostermann, 1972 (*Ausgewählte Schriften* 1).

Wolf, Erik. *Rechtstheologische Studien*, ed. Alexander Hollerbach. Frankfurt am Main: Klostermann, 1972 (*Ausgewählte Schriften* 2).

Wolf, Erik. *Gottesrecht und Nächstenrecht: Rechtstheologische Exegese des Gleichnisses von den Arbeitern im Weinberg (Mt. 20:1–6)*, s.l.: s.n., [1964]. Sonderdruck aus: *Gott in Welt, Festgabe für Karl Kahner zum 60. Geburtstag am 5. März 1964*, eds. Johannes Baptist Metz et al. Vol. 2, 640–662, Freiburg/Basel/Wien: Herder, 1964.

Wolf, Erik. *Ordnung der Liebe: Gottesgebot und Nächstenrecht im Heidelberger Katechismus [Vortrag zur 400-Jahr-Feier des Heidelberger-Katechismus]*. Frankfurt/Main: Klostermann, 1963.

Wolf, Erik. *Ordnung der Kirche: Lehr- und Handbuch des Kirchenrechts auf ökumenischer Basis*. Frankfurt am Main: Vittorio Klostermann, 1961.

Wolf, Erik. *Recht des Nächsten: Ein rechtstheologischer Entwurf*. Frankfurt am Main: Vittorio Klostermann, 1958 (*Philosophische Abhandlungen* XV).

Wolf, Erik. *Rechtsgedanke und biblische Weisung: Drei Vorträge*. Tübingen: Furche-Verlag, [1947] (*Forschungen der Evangelischen Akademie* 5).

Wolf, Erik. *Die Entwicklung des Rechtsbegriffs im reinen Naturrecht*. PhD. diss. Jena. [Jena: s.n.], 1924.

Wolf, Ernst. "Sinn und Grenze der Anwendung der Zwei-Reiche-Lehre auf das Kirchenrecht." In *Staatsverfassung und Kirchenordnung: Festgabe für Rudolf Smend zum 80. Geburtstag am 15. Januar 1962*, eds. K. Hesse, S. Reicke, and U. Scheuner, 443–461. Tübingen: Mohr, 1962.

Wolf, Ernst. "Der christliche Glaube und das Recht: Zu J. Heckel, Lex charitatis." *Zeitschrift für evangelisches Kirchenrecht* 4 (1955): 225–253.

Wolterstorff, Nicholas. *Hearing the Call: Liturgy, Justice, Church, and World*, eds. Mark R. Gornik and Gregory Thompson. Grand Rapids MI/Cambridge UK: Wm.B. Eerdmans, 2011.

Wolterstorff, Nicholas. *Justice in Love*. Grand Rapids MI/Cambridge UK: Wm.B. Eerdmans/, 2011.

Wolterstorff, Nicholas. *Justice: Rights and Wrongs*. Princeton: Princeton University Press, 2008.

Wolterstorff, Nicholas. *Until Justice and Peace Embrace*. Grand Rapids: Eerdmans. 1983. 2nd ed. 1994.

Wolterstorff, Nicholas. *Until Justice and Peace Embrace: The Kuyper Lectures for 1981 delivered at the Free University of Amsterdam*. Grand Rapids, Mich.: W.B. Eerdmans Pub. Co., 1983.

Youtube. "Caritas work in 2022." Accessed 20 March 2024. https://www.youtube.com/watch?time_continue=7&v=7ZormZynGgk&embeds_referring_euri=https%3A%2F%2Fwww.rkkerk.nl%2F&source_ve_path=MTM5MTE3LDM2ODQyLDIzODUx&feature=emb_title.

Printed in the United States
by Baker & Taylor Publisher Services